How to Read the Bible So God Speaks to You

Dr. Noel Enete
Dr. Denise Enete

WAVE
Study
Bible™

Published by Wave Study Bible, Inc.
www.WaveStudyBible.com
Edition 3.0.0

Scripture quotations noted **NIV** are taken from the HOLY BIBLE, NEW INTERNATIONAL VERSION.
Copyright 1973, 1978, and 1984 by International Bible Society. Used by permission of Zondervan Publishing
House. All rights reserved.

Scripture quotations noted **NASB** are taken from the NEW AMERICAN STANDARD BIBLE, Copyright 1960,
1962, 1963, 1968, 1971, 1972, 1973, 1975, 1977, by The Lockman Foundation. Used by permission.

The Four Step Bible study strategy was adapted from Anne Graham Lotz's Living a Life that is Blessed, Copyright 1995 by AnGel Ministries.

Cover by graphic artist and jazz musician Dorothy Collins Wineman, http://www.dotcollins.com.

Comics by concept artist John Enete, http://www.johnenete.com.

ISBN 978-0-9791595-0-3

Printed and bound in the United States of America

Table of Contents

"For I am
the Lord, your God,
who takes hold
of your right hand
and says to you,
'Do not fear;
I will help you.'"

Isa 41:13 (NIV)

Preface

One misty Saturday morning several years ago I [N] was sitting on my surfboard at a local surf spot waiting for a wave with my kids. The surf was small that day and everybody in the water was waiting for the next wave in silence.

When the wave came, I noticed a very small boy, who didn't know how to surf, attempt to catch the wave. He did not know the basics of surfing and was not in the right place to catch the wave nor was he balanced on the surfboard to paddle efficiently. So he missed or got clobbered by most of the waves he tried to catch.

His father stood on the shore—fully clothed and dry. As a wave approached, his father would boom out commands to his struggling son, "Turn around. Paddle! Paddle Harder! You could have gotten that. You've got to try harder!" The father's voice echoed up and down the beach and must have embarrassed the young boy.

After a while, the surfers started exchanging knowing glances of sympathy for the boy's plight. So, I turned to my kids and asked what the father should be doing. They said the father should be in the water—next to his son—helping him succeed rather than shouting commands from a distance.

Many Quiet Time books stand on the shore and shout commands to their struggling readers from a distance. We don't do that. We provide real help.

Just like catching a wave depends on the proper functioning of interrelated skills, developing a successful Bible reading time depends on the balancing of several skills like ①the improvement of your ability to study the Bible, ②the negotiation with your motivation, and ③the management of your time.

Which of these skills to focus on and which to lead with, make all the difference between catching a wave or just getting tired and giving up.

In this journey, we get in the water with you. We help surface the desire God has given you to be with Him. We help you learn to read the Bible in simple steps so God can speak to you. And we help minimize the influences that would push down or choke out your motivation.

By carefully reinforcing your desire for God, at the same time as enhancing your Bible study skill, you will be able to hear and respond to what God says to you.

If you decide to take this journey and do the assignments, rest assured your life will never be the same.

Organization of the Book

The book is divided into two parts and an *Appendix*.

The Book. The first part presents the content of the course in eight chapters. If you are going through this book as a small group, fill-in-the-blank-style note sections are included throughout the chapter so you can take notes while one person reads the chapter aloud to the group. The value for each blank is given in *Appendix C: Answers*.

The Assignments. The second part is a workbook of assignments and space is provided to write the assignment in the book. Included with the assignments is a devotional commentary on the passages you have studied so you can check your work.

The Appendix. The *Appendix* includes an annotated list of Bible study tools, answers to the assignments, a collection of promises you can claim during prayer, a handy reminder card, and additional background information on the authors.

How to Use this Book

As an Individual. If you are going through this book as an individual, go through the eight chapters beginning on page 13 and do the assignments mentioned at the end of each chapter.

As a Small Group. If you are going through this book as a small group, one person could read the chapter aloud and the others could fill in the blanks in the notes sections throughout the chapter. If everyone does the weekly assignment at home, they can discuss what they came up with at the beginning of the next small group meeting. Other groups prefer to do the assignments together during their meeting time.

Acknowledgements

We want to thank my [N] sister, Margaret Conley, for contributing her extensive experience with computer-related Bible tools during the preparation of the software tools section of this volume.

If you have suggestions or simply have benefited from this book, feel free to drop us a note at the address below. Unfortunately, we probably will not be able to reply, but we would love to hear from you.

Drs. Noel and Denise Enete
Carlsbad, California
September 01, 2011

noel.enete@wavestudybible.com
denise.enete@wavestudybible.com
(our last name is pronounced eee NET)

The Book

"Discipline
can smooth out
the bumps in a road,
but it can not
make the road."

The Authors

Chapter 1:
Desire and Discipline

"I think I have to break the door down," Jack blustered.

"Wait! Surely there is another way," his wife countered. But Jack was determined. He had locked them out of their mobile home and was sure this was their only option.

"I'll go around and see if I can get in some other way," his wife offered. But Jack was busy preparing his assault. After a couple of moments, he decided to let it rip and exploded through the front door.

As he lay on the demolished door, his wife came walking down the hall and said dryly, "The back door was open."

I [N] had to laugh when Jack (changed name) recounted the demise of his front door to a group of us. But it is all too common for Christians to take the same approach toward their Bible reading. When their motivation for reading weakens, they think their only option is to mow down their feelings and force themselves through the activity.

If you address your Bible reading the way Jack addressed his front door, it won't be long before you are lying on a demolished time with God. If you are already there, Denise and I are walking down the hall to tell you God provides a better way.

Motivation for Reading

It may surprise you, but the motivation that moves you to read the Bible has a big influence on what you get out of it. At the two extremes, you either sit down to read the Bible because you *want* to *(Desire-led)*, or because you think you *should (Discipline-led)*.

> 1. There are two approaches to having a time with God:
>
> _____ -led
>
> _____ -led

Healthy Bible reading involves both *Desire* and *Discipline* but it is very important which one you lead with.

Bible reading is not the same as doing a homework assignment in school. Usually the objective in school homework is to acquire some information. But the objective in reading the Bible is to enrich your relationship with God and be transformed. *Discipline* is sufficient motivation to acquire facts, but not to change a heart.

Effective Bible reading begins with your motivation.

Desire-led or Discipline-led?

The *Desire-led* approach says the way to read the Bible effectively is to surface and nurture the *Desire* God has given you to be with Him, then read the Bible because you *want* to be a little closer to Him.

Have you ever noticed how much of the Fruit of the Spirit is experiential—love, joy, peace, patience, kindness, goodness, faithfulness, gentleness and self-control *(Galatians 5:22-23)*. Walking with the Lord affects how you *feel*. It is not just a theoretical exercise. It effects the quality of your life.

On the other hand, the *Discipline-led* approach to Bible reading says you can not count on feelings and you should make sure and read your Bible at the scheduled time regardless how you feel. Feelings will follow. Don't make any adjustments to your schedule. Don't make sure the time and frequency match your current *Desire*. Just keep pushing through your Bible reading times regardless.

It is true that sometimes you will not feel like sitting down and spending time with God at the scheduled moment. But if you uncover the *Desire* God has given you, and build your Bible reading time around it, you can get through those rough spots with much less *Discipline*.

Discipline can smooth out the bumps in a road, but it can not build the road.

Although it is not the best strategy, *Discipline-led* Bible reading can work. You might start out with *Discipline*, then get caught up with who God is, along the way, and end up wanting to spend time with Him. But there are hazards with the *Discipline-led* approach.

If you are good at *Discipline*, it is tempting to get a bit smug about regularly checking off Bible reading from your "to do" list when others can't seem to get to theirs. At that point you are operating independently of God. You don't really need God, you are just proudly performing for Him.

On the other hand, if you are *not* good at *Discipline,* you can quickly become disheartened and discouraged because you can't make yourself be consistent.

Surprisingly at that point, I [D] think the disheartened and discouraged person is closer to pleasing God than the smug one. At least the disheartened person knows they need God whereas the proud performer is content to operate independently from Him.

Balanced Bible reading includes *Desire* and *Discipline*. But it is important that you lead with your *Desire*. That is how God equipped you.

Notes

Example: Martha and Mary

The story of Martha and Mary in *Luke 10* contrasts the *Desire-led* and *Discipline-led* approaches to devotion.

For a long time I [D] did not like the story of Martha and Mary in the Bible. Especially around the holidays when I would spend extra time and effort baking, cooking special meals, decorating, and cleaning. I would do these things in service of the family, but it seemed like this Bible passage minimized my efforts. Then God gave me a better understanding of the story. The story is in *Luke 10:38-42*.

> *Luke 10:38-42 As Jesus and his disciples were on their way, he came to a village where a woman named **Martha** opened her home to him. She had a sister called **Mary**, who sat at the Lord's feet listening to what he said. But Martha was distracted by all the preparations that had to be made. She came to him and asked, "Lord, don't you care that my sister has left me to do the work by myself? **Tell her to help me!**" "Martha, Martha," the Lord answered, "you are worried and upset about many things, but only one thing is needed. **Mary has chosen what is better**, and it will not be taken away from her." (NIV)*

You can imagine how Martha and Mary were excited! Jesus was going to be a guest in their home. Martha thought, "Jesus is coming to my home, how can I please Him? I know, I'll make Him a beautiful meal. Then He will know how much I love Him."

On the other hand Mary thought, "Jesus is going to be a guest in our home, how can I please Him? I know. I'll just be with Him. I'll sit at His feet and dote on Him. I'll hang on His every word then He will know how much I love Him."

Martha had more of a *Discipline-led* focus. She was focused on herself—how she could serve and what she could give. Mary was more *Desire-led* with her focus more on Jesus and what she could learn from Him. As we see from the story, Mary had her fingers on Jesus' pulse.

The *Discipline-led* approach to devotion is sort of like a husband who buys his wife tires for her birthday. He is being generous but he probably does not have his fingers on her pulse. Instead, if he were to say, "Your birthday is coming up and I would just love to spend time with you. How about if I take you to a beautiful hotel and just treat you?" Most women would love that gift.

I think the reason the Martha and Mary story made it into the Bible, is that Jesus is a guest in our hearts. How are we going to please Him? Are we going to focus on ourselves and what we can do for Him, or are we going to focus on Him and what we can learn from Him? We will certainly *do* things for Him but where is our focus?

Don't you know that if Martha had gone to Jesus and said, "I'm not sure what to do. I want to make you a beautiful meal, but I also want to be with you. What should I do?" Jesus could have helped her. If He fed 5,000, don't you know He could have handled 12 or so? Martha missed the chance to be with Him.

Notes

Example: Jesus and the Father

Mary is not the only Bible character that lead with their *Desire*. Jesus acts on His *Desire* to be with His Father as described in *Hebrews 1:3,13*.

There are many things that are significant about Jesus sitting at the right hand of the Father, but don't miss the significance of the fellowship they were having. Jesus is spending time just being with the Father.

> *Hebrews 1:3,13 The Son is the radiance of God's glory and the exact representation of his being, sustaining all things by his powerful word. After he had provided purification for sins, he sat down **at the right hand of the Majesty in heaven** ... To which of the angels did God ever say, "**Sit at my right hand** until I make your enemies a footstool for your feet?" (NIV)*

Notes

Deeds and Desire

There is nothing wrong with good works. But leading with them will tend to smother your desire. In *Revelation 2:2-5* God acknowledges the hard work and perseverance of the believers in the church of Ephesus, but He says they have fallen greatly from where they started.

> *Revelation 2:2-5 I know your deeds, **your hard work and your perseverance**. I know that you can not tolerate wicked men, that you have tested those who claim to be apostles but are not, and have found them false. You have persevered and endured hardships for my name, and have not grown weary.*

*Yet I hold this against you: **You have forsaken your first love**. Remember the height from which you have fallen! **Repent and do the things you did at first.** (NIV)*

When they started, they were motivated by love and by *Desiring* a relationship with Him. He urges them to return to being *Desire-led*.

God did not create us for cheap labor, as if He needed our labor *(Acts 17:24-25)*. We are not just worker bees. He could do our work so much faster and more efficiently than we do. But He allows us to blunder along, doing His work, because it is good for us.

> *Acts 17:24-25 "The God who made the world and everything in it is the Lord of heaven and earth and does not live in temples built by hands. **And he is not served by human hands, as if he needed anything,** because he himself gives all men life and breath and everything else." (NIV)*

If you are a parent, and you have a 5 year old child learning to tie his shoes, it is tempting to reach down and tie them when you are in a hurry. But most of the time you wait and let him tie them because it is better for him to practice and learn to do it himself.

God is patient with us. He lets us practice doing things for Him, but He wants us to focus on Him, not on our work for Him. In fact, *Revelation 3:16-21* points out the futility of thinking we are self-sufficient performers. It says rather, that we are blind, pitiful, and poor when we act independently.

> *Revelation 3:16-21 So, because you are lukewarm — neither hot nor cold — I am about to spit you out of my mouth. You say, "I am rich; I have acquired wealth and do not need a thing." But **you do not realize that you are wretched, pitiful, poor, blind and naked.** I counsel you to buy from me gold refined in the fire, so you can become rich; and white clothes to wear, so you can cover your shameful nakedness; and salve to put on your eyes so you can see. Those whom I love I rebuke and discipline. So be earnest, and repent. Here*

*I am! I stand at the door and knock. **If anyone hears my voice and opens the door, I will come in and eat with him, and he with me.** To him who overcomes, I will give the right **to sit with me** on my throne, just as I overcame and **sat down with my Father on his throne.** (NIV)*

We don't need to act independently from God. He offers the fellowship we need. He is willing to let us sit down with Him on His throne.

He has given us a supernatural *Desire* for Him—the Ferrari within. But some of us settle for the tricycle of *Discipline*. We are peddling around as fast as we can, working hard with all the *Discipline* we can muster. But God values fellowship.

In our culture we *are* what we *do*. Our value is in our work. But to God, a quadriplegic is just as valuable as an able-bodied person because fellowship with God is Spirit to spirit not Spirit to resume.

It is all about following your *Desire* to have fellowship with Him.

Notes

God's Desire-led Pattern

It is God's pattern to equip us with the *Desires* we need. God equips an infant with a *Desire* for milk. In *1 Peter 2:2* the Bible says our *Desire* for God is like that baby's *Desire* for milk.

> *1 Peter 2:2* **Like** *newborn babies,* **crave** *pure spiritual milk, so that by it you may grow up in your salvation (NIV)*

If a newborn baby is healthy, he or she *Desires* milk. The baby does not need to use *Discipline* to drink the milk. So think back to when you first accepted God's gift and remember the *Desire* you felt for Him.

Consider the deer in *Psalm 42:1-2* who has a deep, natural, God-given thirst for water. God has placed the same thirst within you.

> *Psalm 42:1-2 As the* **deer pants** *for streams of water, so* **my soul pants for you,** *O God. My soul thirsts for God, for the living God. When can I go and meet with God? (NIV)*

These are God-given *Desires* that keep us on track. Consider the *Desire* God has placed within you. We will help you find that *Desire,* strengthen it, and guard it.

> *Matthew 5:6 Blessed are those who hunger and thirst for righteousness,* **for they will be filled.** *(NIV)*

Notes

Skill Time: Learning to See

Each chapter in this book includes a *Skill Time* segment to help you with one Bible study skill. This enables you to grow your Bible reading skill at the same time you are surfacing your God-given *Desire*. In this *Skill Time* we are focusing on the first step in Bible study.

Out of the four steps in Bible study, the first step is the most important—learning to see.

This single step will do more for your ability to understand the Bible than any other single thing. Bible study is all about what you see. And fortunately, you already know how to do it.

> 2. Bible study is all about what you
>
> SEE _____

We see things all day long. If we see someone frowning and mumbling, we generally conclude they are upset about something. If we see someone smiling and talking quickly with animated gestures, we conclude they are excited. We regularly hone our ability to observe and learn from what we see. This skill is the foundation of all Bible study.

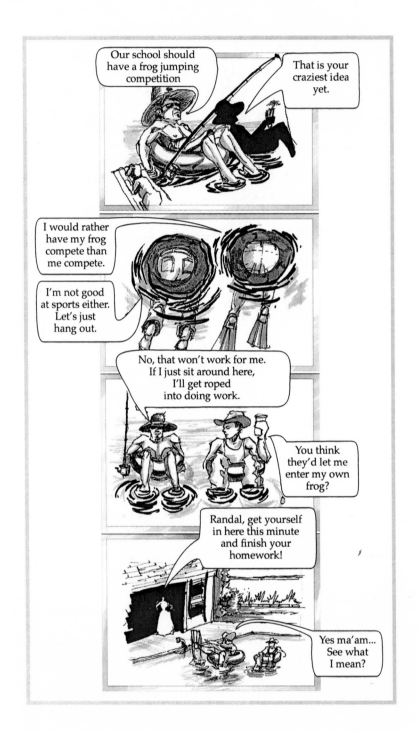

Comic Strip

To take your first step in learning to study the Bible, you will need to find a pen or pencil and get ready to write in the space below.

On the opposite page you will find a comic strip. To help you with the skill of learning to see, take a moment and read the comic. Then simply notice what you see in this comic story and write it down in the space below.

Use short phrases. There are no wrong answers. If you see something, write it down. Just pause for a moment and start writing what you see.

One of them is fishing

Two men sitting on floaters
on the water
One is drinking a cocktail
A woman calling to them
They are in a pool
One had flipper on
They are friends

Students; friends relaxing in water
Not good at sports. Doesn't want to
do work. Maybe calling son to
finish homework

About the Comic Strip

What did you see? If you are stuck and need more help, you can look at the Appendix entitled *Answers* on page 265 for some more suggestions.

Did you happen to notice that the two boys' clothing implied the weather was probably hot.

Did you notice the way these two boys talked to each other? They were probably friends and their appearance indicated they were probably High School age.

They were talking about frog jumping and they both had pet frogs which may imply they lived in a rural area.

What do you suppose their social standing was with their peers? Since neither one was good at sports and they liked hanging out by themselves, they were probably on the social fringe.

What do you make out of the flippers that one boy was wearing? What do you make out of the hats they were wearing?

Consider for a moment, how much you surfaced from this simple comic after only a few moments of looking at it. You have a sense for the boys' personality, their social standing, their environment, and what life is like in their world.

You got all of this information by simply looking and writing down what you saw. This is the same skill used in Bible study.

Bible Passage

The first step in Bible study is just like what you did with the comic.

You will find a couple of sentences from the Bible below. Read the sentences, then in the space below them, write out what you see.

It will only take a few seconds. Pause and begin writing what you see. For now, don't worry about being right or wrong. We will deal with that in a later chapter. For now, write down whatever you see.

> *1 John 4:18 There is no fear in love; but perfect love casts out fear, because fear involves punishment, and the one who fears is not perfected in love.*
>
> *1 John 4:19 We love, because He first loved us. (NASB)*

One thing the author is talking about is love
There is a contrast between
fear & love.
There is a concept of perfect
love
Perfect love = no fear
Our love results from this
love
Punishment = fear
God loved us first

About the Bible Passage

What did you see? If you find yourself stuck and need more examples, you can check the Appendix entitled *Answers* on page 265.

Did you happen to notice that the author was talking about love and fear? Did you see the presence of one of these excludes the other?

What did you see in the phrase "involves punishment?" What did you see in the phrase relating our love and God's love?

Though this is only the first step in Bible study, look at how much you have pulled from the passage by simply writing down what you see.

Bible study is all about what you see. With your two eyes you are fully equipped to surface what God has to say to you.

If you are interested in exploring further the skill of seeing, there is an appendix entitled *How Well do You See* on page 275.

Assignment 1

At the end of each chapter is an assignment that should take less than an hour to complete. If you want this material to make a difference in your life, get comfortable and give this assignment a try.

If you get stuck doing the assignment and need more suggestions, more are available in the Appendix titled *Answers* on page 265.

For Your Heart

Take the first step toward uncovering your desire for God by meditating on the verses on page 22: *1 Peter 2:2, Psalm 42:1-2,* and *Matthew 5:6.* As you do, start thinking about your own desire for God. Pray that, over time, you will be able to uncover and strengthen it.

Like newborn babies, crave pure spiritual milk, so that by it you may grow up in your salvation, now that you have tasted that the Lord is good. PETER 2:2

As the deer pants for streams of water, so my soul pants for you, O God. My soul pants for God, for the living God. Where can I go and meet with God? PSALM 42:1-2

Blessed are those who hunger & thirst for righteousness, for they will be filled.

For Your Mind

The passage below is taken from *Philippians 1*. Using the space below the passage, write what you see in *this* passage. Remember to use short phrases and just surface what you can see.

Philippians 1:9 And this I pray, that your love may abound still more and more in real knowledge and all discernment,

Philippians 1:10 so that you may approve the things that are excellent, in order to be sincere and blameless until the day of Christ;

Philippians 1:11 having been filled with the fruit of righteousness which [comes] through Jesus Christ, to the glory and praise of God. (NASB)

The author wants their love to increase.

Want real knowledge + discernment
Want them to be sincere &
without blame

"A pencil
is the crowbar
of the mind."

Dr. Howard Hendricks

"Blessed are those
who hunger and thirst
for righteousness,
for they will be filled."

Matthew 5:6 (NIV)

Chapter 2:
Surfacing your Desire

I [N] felt nervous as I stood in the Dallas Theological Seminary bookstore. In a few short weeks I would enter the school as a first year student and I had some serious doubts about my ability to succeed in a program so demanding—especially since my background was engineering and the study of the Bible was basically a liberal arts curriculum.

In engineering, most assignments involved reading a few pages from the book and working out several pages of problems. In DTS, I would be required to read thousands of pages and write several long papers each week.

I knew I needed help with my reading skill so I selected the book *How to Read a Book* from the bookstore. I figured that should take care of things. Then after I took it home and started reading, I noticed the book was over 400 pages long and school started in a few weeks. So I went back to the bookstore and bought the book *How to Read Better and Faster* so I could get through *How to Read a Book.*

The first day of classes arrived and I began the legendary workload. During the first week I got the assignments for the semester for all my classes and spread them out, as best I could, on a large chart then sat back and shuddered. This was too much work. According to my estimates I would need to study 200 hours each week to keep up.

Denise and I both studied the chart trying to decide what to do. It was clear that God called me to help others study the Bible and DTS had the best program to prepare me for that, but I had to face the looming possibility that I could fail at this.

Then Denise suggested a novel idea. She said this was too much work not to enjoy. "What about just doing what you want to do? If you want to study, then study, if not, then don't. If you want to study a particular subject, then study it, if not, then don't. Let your *Desire* be the guide for what you do and how much you do it. That way, even if you fail, you still get what you wanted from the program."

This sounded like science fiction. I had a natural interest in some of the courses like Greek and Hebrew. But other courses I did not like at all. In one course I needed to explore the oblique process of dating pottery from an archeological site. Plus, my performance in school had only been average up to that point, and I could not see how backing off the push would give me *any* chance of success.

Then something amazing happened. When I consulted what I *wanted* to do, I discovered that a surprising amount of the time I wanted to be responsible.

Encouraged by that, I looked at the courses I did not like, to see if there was anything I wanted to learn from them. Surprisingly, when I took this approach I discovered that it was an interesting puzzle to try and guess the age of a piece of pottery given the little bit of information we have to go on. As I surfaced things I wanted to get from my least favorite courses I was surprised to discover what *I* wanted from the course was not far from what the *professor* wanted me to know.

Once I was in touch with what I wanted to do, creativity came out of nowhere and went to work on the 200 hours per week. I found and interviewed people who were good students and learned what worked for them. I learned how to take better notes in class and how to spend less time studying for tests in content classes. I made sure to give the majority of my time to my favorite courses and figured out ways to do the efficient minimum on classes I liked the least.

After all the dust settled, my schedule was possible—all because it was something I wanted to do.

Make no mistake, following my *Desire* did not guarantee success. In fact, sometimes when there was a lot of pressure and I did not want to study, the idea of following my *Desire* seemed to work against me.

But, in a very surprising way, following my *Desire* put me in *the best place* to succeed because it got me running at peak efficiency, with peak creativity and a positive attitude. It told me when I needed rest and it told me when I could successfully push. The amount of *Discipline* I needed to get through the rough spots felt reasonable since it was in service of accomplishing what I wanted to do.

Your *Desire* is your most effective tool in negotiating a collection of conflicting requirements. There is no more effective arbitrator regardless of your personality. *Desire* helps the hard driving person not burn out. *Desire* helps the free spirit focus without feeling forced.

But *Desire* does not live in a vacuum. Your deepest and truest *Desires* live in the same space as your shallow and passing *Desires* and with things that seem like *Desires* but are not.

How can you distinguish your true *Desires* from the others? Your true *Desires* surface when you minimize the *Desire Killers* and get a clear fix on what you want the most.

Desire Killer: Deceitful Desires

As seen in *Chapter 1*, God wants us to surface our *Desire* for Him and follow it. But as we do, He is careful to warn us about influences that can undermine our *Desire*.

We are warned about the first *Desire Killer* in *Ephesians 4:22-23*.

> *Ephesians 4:22-23 You were taught, with regard to your former way of life, to put off your old self, which is being corrupted by its **deceitful desires**; to be made new in the attitude of your minds; (NIV)*

What are *Deceitful Desires*? *Deceit* is the misrepresentation of truth, that is, a lie. But how could a *Desire* be a lie?

1. Deceit means

    _____A   LIE_____

A *Desire* lies when it promises fulfillment but does not deliver. When a *Desire* says that you will be fulfilled if you just go shopping, eating, traveling, gambling, exercising, sleeping, watching TV, playing sports, buying gadgets, reading romance novels, or burying yourself in work, that is a *Deceitful Desire*. When a *Desire* promises fulfillment but does not deliver, it is *Deceitful*.

2. A *Deceitful Desire* is a *Desire* that promises fulfillment but

    _____DOES NOT DELIVER_____

When I [D] feel empty or bored, my *Deceitful Desire* of choice is shopping. I think if I just go shopping, I'll feel better. I'll feel some success, because I'll get a cute outfit. I won't torch the budget, and will have succeeded at something. I'll be a good shopper with good taste (and I do feel better for awhile). However, this is a *Deceitful Desire* for me because <u>at the end of my life I won't look back and decide my life had meaning because I got a lot of cute outfits.</u>

Following *Deceitful Desires* is like taking emotional anesthesia. It numbs your pain for a while, but like anesthesia, it wears off. If we keep running to the refrigerator, the mall, or the TV for comfort, we never develop the path to God for comfort.

3. If we keep fulfilling *Deceitful Desires,* we never develop

_THE PATH TO GOD_____ for comfort.

A Grandfather told this Parable of the Wolves to his Grandson:

"There are two wolves living in my heart and they are at war with each other. One is vicious and cruel and the other is wise and kind."

"Grandfather," said the alarmed grandson, "which one will win?"

"The one I feed," said the Grandfather.

We all have well-worn paths to what we think is our help. If our help is *Deceitful*, it is a *Desire Killer* and will lead us away from finding the help God provides.

But you say, "It can't always be wrong to shop or buy a gadget." You are right. It is often very normal and healthy to do some of these things.

How do you know when a *Desire* is an appropriate comfort and when it is *Deceitful*? The *Desire* becomes *Deceitful* when you rely on it to bring fulfillment or when you consistently rely on it to numb you.

---

4. A *Desire* becomes *Deceitful* when you rely on it to bring

FULFILLMENT or when you rely on it to

NUMB YOU

God does not want you to continually escape. He wants you to experience comfort right where you are. God's comfort keeps you in the moment and connects you to Him in the midst of the situation. It is a strange mixture of joy and sadness. Dr. James Dobson says, "God does not give us a detour from problems, but a guided tour through them."

The Old Testament character David was clear that God was the answer for comfort. Look how many times David says "you" in *Psalm 63:1-8*.

> *Psalm 63:1-8   O God, **you** are my God, earnestly I seek **you**; my soul thirsts for **you**, my body longs for **you**, in a dry and weary land where there is no water.*
>
> *I have seen **you** in the sanctuary and beheld **your** power and your glory. Because **your** love is better than life, my lips will glorify **you**. I will praise **you** as long as I live, and in **your** name I will lift up my hands. My soul will be satis-*

fied as with the richest of foods; with singing lips my mouth will praise **you.**

On my bed I remember **you;** *I think of* **you** *through the watches of the night. Because* **you** *are my help, I sing in the shadow of* **your** *wings. My soul clings to* **you;** **your** *right hand upholds me. (NIV)*

David is not turning to *Deceitful Desires* for comfort. He is clear that the answer is not on earth. The earth is a dry and weary land.

David was receiving comfort from God. He said God's love was better than life and satisfied him just like the richest of foods. Visualize biting into the most delicious food you have ever tasted. Can you picture your reaction? Does your head go back with your eyes closed? David is saying his experience with God is like that. His soul clings to God and is comforted.

5. Rather than turning to *Deceitful Desires*, David received comfort

BY CLINGING TO GOD

As you surface and begin following your deepest and truest *Desires*, be aware that you will also encounter *Desires* that seem to promise fulfillment but do not deliver. Instead they bury or distract us from the *Desire* God has given us.

The Parable of the Wolf implies that the *Desire* we feed will grow stronger. What *Desire* are you feeding? If we only go to the refrigerator, the car lot, the mall, the TV, or work we could be feeding a *Deceitful Desire*.

6. The *Desire* you feed will

GROW
_____

What Do You Want?

But, how can we find our *Desire* for God? I [D] found my *Desire* for God by pondering the following seven questions for a few months.

1. Do I want to know God?

2. How do I want my life to be?

3. Do I want to do His will for my life?

4. Do I want to please God?

5. Do I want to know His heart and what He cares about?

6. Would I prefer my independence over His will and way?

7. It might change my priorities. What do I really want?

Answering these questions for yourself is part of the assignment at the end of this chapter. Be honest as you answer them. See where you hesitate. Notice your reactions. This is like taking your spiritual temperature.

You don't have to tell anyone which questions made you uncomfortable. Although if you did, you would find you are not alone, and that is always encouraging for both people.

Being honest with yourself will enable you to see where you are hesitating. Do you have trouble with the questions that encourage you to know God and please Him? Or is your hesitation more centered around giving up your independence in exchange for His guidance? Are you worried that He will ruin your life if you give it to Him?

Noticing where you hesitate gives you valuable information. If your Christian walk sputters unevenly along, knowing where you might be stuck will help you know where to put your effort to smooth things out.

7. Answering honestly helps you see where you are

HESITATING

If you don't face your hesitations squarely, you may wonder why you are always stepping on the gas then putting on the brake in your walk with Christ.

Ultimately, facing our hesitations squarely and addressing them, gives us the ability to put our foot on the gas and keep it there. God has given His children a *Desire* for Him. Our job is to nurture that *Desire* so it grows.

8. Facing your hesitations helps you know where to place your

EFFORT TO SMOOTH THINGS OUT

Skill Time: Four Step Bible Study

The *Skill Time* in *Chapter 1* introduced the first and most important step in Bible study—learning to see. This time we will cover all four steps in devotional Bible study.

Don't be worried if the steps do not make perfect sense at first. Give it some time. Most people have trouble with the steps at first, but you'll catch on after you practice the assignments for a while. You will be glad you hung in there.

Let's begin with a review of the first step.

Facts

The first step, which we called *Learning to See* in *Chapter 1*, is also called gathering the *Facts*. This is the step where you simply list what you see. These are the *Facts* of the passage. It is OK to use the same words the passage uses when you write out the *Facts*. You are just writing short phrases that identify what you see.

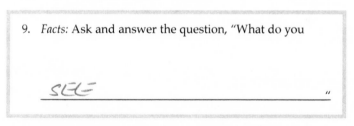

9. *Facts:* Ask and answer the question, "What do you

SEE "

Be careful not to decide either way about whether you understand the passage or not. Rather, withhold judgement and continue to identify things you see.

> 10. Instead of concluding that you understand or don't understand the passage,
>
> *IDENTIFY THINGS you SEE*

Frequently something will catch your attention that you do not understand. Resist the temptation to spend all your time trying to figure it out. Rather, focus on what you *can* see and you will be surprised how many of the other things get cleared up.

> 11. Write down what you *can*
>
> *SEE*

Sometimes you may look at a passage and draw a total blank. If that should happen, ask yourself the *Who, What, Where, When, Why,* questions about the passage. "*Who* is the passage talking about?" "*Where* are they?" "*Why* are they doing this?" "*When* do these events occur?"

If questions occur to you as you are studying the passage, write them in the *Facts* panel along with the other things you see. We will address answering your questions in *Chapter 4.*

On the following pages I [N] would like you to try your hand at surfacing the *Facts* in *Genesis 11:26-12:1*. Take a look at the passage and write what you see in the *Facts* panel on the following page. Aim to write down at least three or four *Facts*.

After you write what you see, compare your *Facts* with the *Facts* on the following page. I do not expect you to have this many *Facts*. But these are listed so you get a feel for what a *Fact* is. Why don't you take a moment and give it a try.

Bible Passage

Genesis 11:26 After Terah had lived 70 years, he became the father of Abram, Nahor and Haran.

Genesis 11:27 This is the account of Terah. Terah became the father of Abram, Nahor and Haran. And Haran became the father of Lot.

Genesis 11:28 While his father Terah was still alive, Haran died in Ur of the Chaldeans, in the land of his birth.

Genesis 11:29 Abram and Nahor both married. The name of Abram's wife was Sarai, and the name of Nahor's wife was Milcah; she was the daughter of Haran, the father of both Milcah and Iscah.

Genesis 11:30 Now Sarai was barren; she had no children.

Genesis 11:31 Terah took his son Abram, his grandson Lot son of Haran, and his daughter-in-law Sarai, the wife of his son Abram, and together they set out from Ur of the Chaldeans to go to Canaan. But when they came to Haran, they settled there.

Genesis 11:32 Terah lived 205 years, and he died in Haran.

Genesis 12:1 The Lord had said to Abram, "Leave your country, your people and your father's household and go to the land I will show you. (NIV)

1. Facts

List what you see in the passage

Terah fathered Abram, Nahor and Haran after he turned 70.

Terah is Abram, Nahor & Haran's father.

Haram is Lot's father

Haran died in UR, he was born there

Haran's children - Milcah & Iscah

Abram married Sarai

Nahor married Milah

Sarai was barren

Terah, Abram, Lot, Sarai left for Canaan.

They settled in Haran

Terah died in Haran

Terah was 205 years

Lord told Abram to leave his fathers family

Lord said he will tell him where to go.

Nahor married his niece

1. Facts

List what you see in the passage

Terah fathered Abram, Nahor and Haran after he turned 70.

Terah fathered Abram, Nahor and Haran.

Haran fathered Lot.

Haran died in Ur of Chaldeans.

Abram married Sarai.

Nahor married Milcah.

Milcah was Haran's daughter.

Iscah was Haran's daughter.

Sarai was barren.

Terah took his son Abram and wife Sarai, and grandson Lot and left Ur of Chaldeans to go to Canaan, but settled at Haran.

Terah died in Haran at 205 yrs old.

God tells Abram to leave his country to go to the land God will show him.

Lessons

After you surface the *Facts,* the next step is to determine the *Lessons* that can be learned from the *Facts.* What is God teaching me here? Is there a command to obey, a warning to heed, a promise to hold on to, a comfort to enjoy, or an action that sheds light on God's personality and values? If so, that is a *Lesson* and should be written in this panel.

12. *Lessons:* Ask and answer the question, "What can be

LEARNT FROM THE PASSAGE "

To find a *Lesson,* sometimes it is helpful to ask yourself what you find unusual or what stands out to you in the passage. Then figure out a way to express that and see if you can learn something from it. If so, you have found a *Lesson* and write it in the *Lessons* panel.

13. To find a *Lesson* ask yourself what in the passage is the most

UNUSUAL or STANDS OUT

14. Then figure out how to express it and see if you can

LEARN SOMETHING FROM IT

Think about the *Facts* you surfaced in the last step and make a guess or two about what could be learned from this current passage and write it in the *Lessons* panel on the next page.

For example, one of the things we can learn from the *Fact* that Terah fathered his most famous children after he was 70 years old, is that our greatest purposes for God can be accomplished late in life.

After you write your guess, compare your *Lessons* with the *Lessons* on the following page. I do not expect you to have this many *Lessons*. In fact, you normally only come up with one or two *Lessons* in a Bible reading time. The extra ones are given so you get the idea what a *Lesson* is.

This can be the trickiest of the *Four Steps* in Bible study so be patient with yourself and just give it your best guess. We will have more to say about the *Lessons* step in *Chapter 3* but for now, look at the *Facts* and write out your best guess or two in the *Lessons* panel about what can be learned from *Genesis 11:26-12:1*.

2. Lessons

We can accomplish our greatest purpose for God in our later years.

God talks to people

God may not tell you
where he wants you
to go.

2. Lessons

Write down what you learn from this passage

We can accomplish our greatest purpose for God in our later years.

God unveils His will gradually sometimes. (Genesis 12:1)

When God asks us to do something He wants us to trust Him and be willing to step out without knowing all the facts.

Sarai was barren, but it was according to God's purpose.

Challenges

The next step is to turn each *Lesson* into a question that *Challenges* your life. Write the questions in the *Challenges* panel on the next page. If you surfaced two *Lessons*, you should come up with two questions here.

15. *Challenges:* Ask and answer the question, "Where does it touch

_____ "

16. You should have as many *Challenges* as you have

_____

You are asking yourself how your life squares with each of the *Lessons* you surfaced. The purpose of these questions is *not* to evoke guilt. The purpose is to identify and explore potential ways the truth of the passage touches your life.

Give it a try in the *Challenges* panel on the next page.

Response

Now, in the last step of Bible study, sit back and consider what you have surfaced and how it touches your life and listen for what God might be saying to you. God does not always have something to say, but He often does. Listen for Him.

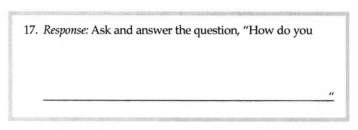

17. *Response:* Ask and answer the question, "How do you

_____ "

Consider how you *Respond* to what God is saying and write it in the *Response* panel. This usually takes the form of a two or three sentence prayer to God.

Don't be overly ambitious in your response. Be honest. Don't promise the moon when you know you won't be able to deliver it. This is not a sprint, it is a walk. Ask for help in making the *Lessons* and *Challenges* part of your life. If God is asking you to do something you don't want to do, don't be afraid to respond by asking Him to help *you want* what *He wants.*

3. Challenges

Turn the lessons into questions that challenge you

Do I think it is too late for God to use me?

Is God talking to me?

4. Response

Listen to what God is saying to you and write out your response

Lord please let me hear you talking to me. Thanks for telling me that I not too old for your purpose.

3.   Challenges

Turn the lessons into questions that challenge you

Do I think it is too late for God to use me?

Am I willing to move out without all the information if God directs?

Am I trusting God with the barren issues in my life?

4.   Response

Listen to what God is saying to you and write out your response

Lord, please help me follow Your purpose for me, even if I don't understand everything.

Please help me trust you with the barren issues in my life.

Assignment 2

There are two parts to this assignment and should take no more than an hour combined.

For Your Mind

Study *Passage 1* in the *Abraham Workbook* on page 204. Fill in the four panels as discussed in this chapter.

After you have worked on *Passage 1,* if you want some more ideas, take a look at the Appendix titled *Answers* on page 265. But be sure to give the assignment a try first.

For Your Heart

Get quiet each day for several days and answer these questions for yourself each time:

1. Do I want to know God?

2. How do I want my life to be?

3. Do I want to do His will for my life?

4. Do I want to please God?

5. Do I want to know His heart and what He cares about?

6. Would I prefer my independence over His will and way?

7. It might change my priorities. What do I really want?

You are taking your spiritual temperature so be honest when answering these questions. See where you hesitate. If you are honest about where you put on the brakes, then you can do something about it. If you don't face your hesitations squarely, you may wonder why you are always stepping on the gas then putting on the brake in your walk with the Lord.

"Listen for what
God might be saying
to you."

The Authors

"For as he thinks
within himself,
so is he."

Prov 23:7a (NASB)

Chapter 3:
Renewing Your Mind

As I [N] dove into the pool, I remember being nervous about jumping into the water with these monsters. It was the beginning of my second year of High School and this was my first varsity water polo game.

I had watched the varsity play the previous year while I was on the junior team and marveled at how fast and powerful they were. But after diving in and taking my position in the game, I was amazed how big they were. As the game progressed I had trouble keeping up with my man and was getting pushed around the pool.

Then at half-time, the coach pulled me aside and said, "You are just as big and fast as anyone out there. Now get back in there and don't let anyone get past you." I remember looking at the other players, then looking at myself and being surprised that my coach might be right.

Between my first and second year of High School, I had a dramatic growth spurt in which I gained 20 pounds and several inches of height. My second year sprint times were greatly improved and I had much more overall strength. But I had not updated my thinking.

After half-time I took the coach's advice and, to my surprise, I discovered that I *was* just as fast and just as powerful as anyone out there. For the rest of the game, no one got past me.

What was different in the second half? Had I suddenly become stronger and faster? No, the only thing that changed was my thinking.

The battle is won or lost in our mind.

How We Think Effects How We feel

Even if we are not aware of it, we are always thinking. And our thoughts effect us in profound ways. You may be surprised to hear that our thoughts move our feelings. Consider the following examples.

Elevator example

Let us suppose a group of people are trapped in an elevator. You would think they would leave the elevator having a similar feeling since they all experienced the same crisis. But that is not how it works.

About a fourth of the people will leave the elevator angry. The whole time they are trapped they are thinking about how they have been inconvenienced. They worry about being late for an appointment and they want to know why the building doesn't maintain their elevators properly.

A fourth will leave the elevator anxious. The whole time they are trapped they are thinking about the safety issues. What if the cable breaks and they plunge down to the basement or what if they run out of oxygen? They rehearse in their mind all of the dangers and so they become anxious.

A fourth will leave excited. While they are trapped, they are planning who they will call to tell about the man who was freaking out or the lady who was so mad. For them, the experience is material to entertain their friends.

The last fourth don't give it much thought. They just wait patiently. They aren't thinking about the inconvenience or safety issues and they don't even mention it to anyone. It is just not that important. They leave the elevator unaffected.

All of these people were trapped on an elevator. But what they were thinking about determined how they ended up feeling.

Job example

Now consider how you would feel if you lost your job.

If you tell yourself, "They have no right to fire me," you will be angry. If you say "I am such a loser, I can't do anything right," you will feel sad.

But if you say, "Well, this isn't the time I would have chosen, but I have been wanting to try something else and now I can," you will feel nervous, but excited for the chance for change.

It is likely that you will cycle through all these thoughts and that is why you feel like a mess—cycling through anger, sadness, excitement, and fear.

Example of Fred

For the final example, let's say we go to a party and I introduce you to Fred. As Fred talks to you, he looks over your shoulder and across the room. At that point, your feelings will be determined by how you interpret his behavior.

If you say to yourself, "Fred is so rude," you will be irritated. If you say, "I bore everyone," you will feel sad. If you say, "Fred seems socially awkward, I wonder if he is shy," you will probably feel some compassion for his discomfort.

People who are continually angry, tend to interpret the events around them as personal insults. Those who are determined to be depressed, see the events around them as evidence of their failure. Neither tune in to the possibility that Fred might be rude or shy due to his own pain.

A Test of Thinking

Victor Frankl was held in the Aushewitz prison camp but he kept his spirits up by realizing his captors could take his family and his life, but they couldn't take away his hope to find meaning even in tragic situations.

After Jesus died on the cross, the disciples had a test of their thinking. When they found Jesus' body missing from the tomb, they had a choice. Some chose to interpret Jesus's missing body as a disaster, but in *John 20:8-9* John chose to believe.

> *John 20:8-9 Finally the other disciple, who had reached the tomb first, also went inside. He saw and* **believed**. *(They still did not understand from Scripture that Jesus had to rise from the dead.) (NIV)*

What miracle in your life are you thinking is a disaster? Jesus's death on the cross looked like a huge disaster. Jesus came to be the king of the Israelites but they killed him. It looked like a failure. Looks can be deceiving. What looked like a failure was actually the biggest victory in the history of mankind.

In each of these examples, the person's feelings depended on what they were thinking. But you may say, "I don't know what I am thinking during the day." Yes, that is often the case.

But, there are a few times during the day when most of us tune in to what we are thinking. One is when the alarm clock goes off. We debate the pros and cons of getting up on time. Another time is the great "should I have one more cookie" debate. We tune in for that too.

1. One time we tune in to what we are thinking is when

THE ALARM CLOCK GOES OFF

Or when debating if we should have another

ANOTHER COOKIE

It is possible to tune in to what we are thinking at other times as well. If you want to change your heart and soul, change comes through your mind. That is why the Bible is in written form.

How We Think Effects How We Grow

Our thoughts spiritually transform us. The Bible describes spiritual change as beginning in our mind.

> 2. Our thoughts spiritually
>
> _BEGINS WITH THE MIND_

Before we accepted the forgiveness of sins, *Ephesians 2:3* indicates we were following the *thoughts* of our sinful nature.

> Ephesians 2:3 *All of us also lived among them at one time, gratifying the cravings of our sinful nature and following its desires and **thoughts**... (NIV)*

> 3. Before salvation, our thoughts led us
>
> _TO SIN_

After we accepted the forgiveness of sins, our continuing *Transformation* comes from a renewed *mind*. according to *Romans 12:2*.

> Romans 12:2 *Do not conform any longer to the pattern of this world, but be transformed by the **renewing of your mind**. Then you will be able to test and approve what God's will is—his good, pleasing and perfect will. (NIV)*

4. After salvation, our thoughts

ARE TRANSFORMED BY THE MIND

In both situations our spiritual direction is a result of what we are thinking about. God's design for change begins in our *minds (Philippians 2:5).*

> Philippians 2:5 Let this **mind** be in you, which was also in Christ Jesus: (KJV)

God is calling for a mind transplant. He did not say "Let this heart be in you" because hearts are broken at times. He wants our minds so we can be steadfast. It is very clear. We are not transformed by obedience. God says let His Word renew your mind, then you will approve His will and likely do it. *(Romans 12:2)*

5. God is calling for a

MIND TRANSPLANT

How does our mind transform us to be more like God? By thinking about things from God's point of view. What kind of things should we be thinking about? The Bible gives us an excellent starting place in *Philippians 4:8.*

> Philippians 4:8 Finally, brothers, whatever is *true,* whatever is *noble,* whatever is *right,* whatever is *pure,* whatever is *lovely,* whatever is *admirable*—if anything is *excellent* or *praiseworthy*—**think about** such things. (NIV)

6. We are transformed by thinking about things

FROM GOD'S POINT OF VIEW

If your friend says "Come on, lets watch this movie where the whole family gets hacked to pieces. It's a true story and we need to know what goes on." Would this fit the *Philippians 4:8* test? It might be true but it doesn't fit the noble, pure, or lovely criteria.

Does that mean we are to just blow sunshine around all the time and not be in reality? No, this verse says to think on things that are "true." So stay in reality. But shift to the way God sees it. There is hope in God's reality.

The Bible presents our thoughts as the battle ground where all is won or lost. Paul describes his strategy for guiding what he thinks about in *2 Corinthians 10:5*.

> *2 Corinthians 10:5 We demolish arguments and every pretension that sets itself up against the knowledge of God, and we **take captive every thought** to make it obedient to Christ. (NIV)*

When I [D] first read this verse it seemed overwhelming. How can a person take captive *every* thought?

Then I realized this is telling us what to do with renegade thoughts that argue against the knowledge of God. A renegade thought is a thought like, "That isn't fair," "that was harsh," or "that was wrong." If you find yourself beginning to judge God, you are to take *that* thought captive. You make that thought obedient to Christ. You refuse to judge God when you don't have all the information. It is a test.

7. We are to "take captive"

EVERY THOUGHT

How We Think Effects What We Want

The strategy we have found helpful for surfacing the *Desire* God gave us for Him has two parts.

First, it is helpful to answer the seven questions on page 41. This helps you make a realistic appraisal of the current strength of your desire.

Then it helps to pray the following three passages back to God. These passages help you grasp the kindness God has shown to you and respond in kind. Together they help you gently nudge your desire forward.

In the first passage, *Ephesians 3:16-19,* Paul asks God to give the Christians in Ephesus power so they are able to grasp God's love for them.

> *Ephesians 3:16-19 I pray that out of his glorious riches he may strengthen you with power through his Spirit in your inner being, so that Christ may dwell in your hearts through faith.*
>
> *And I pray that you, being rooted and established in love,* **may have power**, *together with all the saints,* **to grasp how wide and long and high and deep is the love of Christ**, *and to know this love that surpasses knowledge—that you may be filled to the measure of all the fullness of God. (NIV)*

This is something we can also pray for. Here is the same verse arranged as your prayer to God.

"Father I pray that out of Your glorious riches You would strengthen me with power through Your Spirit in my inner being, so that Christ may dwell in my heart through faith.

And I pray that You would root and establish me in this love, so that I may have the power to grasp how wide and long and high and deep is Your love for me, and to know Your love which surpasses knowledge—that I may be filled to the measure of all Your fullness.

Take your time. Ask God to help you. Come back to this verse over and over asking for help and watching for God to help you grasp His love.

Notes

The second passage, *Mark 12:30-31,* helps us respond to His love as we begin to understand it.

> *Mark 12:30-31 "'**Love the Lord your God** with all your **heart** and with all your **soul** and with all your **mind** and with all your **strength**.' The second is this: 'Love your neighbor as yourself.' There is no commandment greater than these."*

First notice that it says you are to love your neighbor as you love yourself. Raise your hand if you love yourself perfectly. No one loves themselves perfectly. The idea is to do the best you can. Those who are aware how much God loves and forgives them, will be better at loving and forgiving their neighbor. The ultimate goal is to love and forgive the way God does.

Next, notice the dimensions of our response. We are to love God with our mind, strength, heart, and soul. What does that look like?

How do we love God with our mind? Loving God with our mind means that we think the way God wants us to think. How do we interpret what goes on in our life? Do we value the things God values? Do we think about things the way God thinks about them?

It also says to love God with our strength. What does strength imply? Our strength enables our actions and by them our behavior. We should love God by the way we behave.

How do we love God with our heart? The heart is the seat of our feelings. Are our emotions ruled by faith and trust, or by hatred and bitterness, for example.

How do we love God with our soul? The Bible uses heart and soul interchangeably at times. But, the soul stands for the living being. *"God breathed into his nostrils the breath of life and man became a living soul." (Genesis 2:7 KJV)* The soul is what leaves the body at death and goes to be with God. It is who we are apart from our body.

It is helpful to pray this passage back to God and ask Him to help move us in this direction. Here is the passage arranged as a prayer to God.

> "Father I pray that You will help me to love You with all my heart and with all my soul and with all my mind and with all my strength, and help me to love my neighbor as myself because this is what You want most for me."

Notes

The third passage, *Luke 18:13b*, helps to round out our perspective. It is already arranged as a prayer to God, so you can pray it directly to God.

> *Luke 18:13b 'God, have mercy on me, a sinner.' (NIV)*

This is helpful in a couple of ways. It grounds you if you are proud because you may be thinking you love God more than you actually do. It also gives hope to the weary and unsure person because they focus too intently on how short their love falls.

Praying these three passages back to God and pondering the seven questions will help you surface the desire God has given you for Him. Don't rush it. Keep coming back to these questions and passages from time to time. The process of restoring your desire may take some time, but it gets the horse back in front of the cart and empowers all of your time with God.

Notes

Desire Killer: Futile Thinking

If our thinking effects us in profound ways, it only stands to reason that certain kinds of thinking can effect us in negative ways. In *Ephesians 4:17* God cautions us to avoid *Futile Thinking*.

> *Ephesians 4:17 So I tell you this, and insist on it in the Lord, that you must no longer live as the Gentiles do, in the **futility of their thinking**. (NIV)*

8. God cautions us to avoid

   FUTILE THINKING

What is *Futile Thinking?* The word *Futile* implies that something is useless, vain, or that it leads nowhere. It is thinking that does not bear fruit. *Futile Thoughts* are *Thoughts* that lead you nowhere like "He who dies with the most toys wins," or "what happens in Las Vegas stays in Las Vegas."

9. *Futile Thoughts* lead you

   TO NOWHERE

Futile Thinking and *Deceitful Desires* (cf. page 35) are both *Desire Killers*. Rather than strengthening your walk with God, they lead away from God. They focus your attention on substitutes for God that either promise help without delivering it or get you to espouse agreement with nonsensical ideas.

As you ponder the seven questions on page 41, it is important to notice places where you hesitate. Because those may be places where a *Desire Killer* is at work.

For example, if you hesitate on question three, "Do I want to do His will for my life," you might worry that God's will may interfere with a futile goal like wanting to die "with the most toys." Or, if you hesitate on question one, "Do I want to know God," you may worry that knowing God will interfere with some television watching—which could be a *Deceitful Desire* in that it promises rest and refreshment and often ends up fatiguing you.

As you continue pondering the seven questions, notice where you hesitate. Hesitations point you to what may be holding you back so you can do something about it.

Skill Time: Finding the Lesson

Skill Time in the last chapter was probably your first exposure to *Four Step Bible Study*. Don't be worried if the steps are not completely clear. That is the case for most people right now. Hang in there and you will get it.

While the first step, gathering the *Facts*, is the most important step, the second step, surfacing the *Lessons*, is the most difficult step. It is not always obvious what can be learned from the *Facts* of the passage. This *Skill Time* will give you more ideas how to surface the *Lessons*.

---

10. The most difficult step in Bible study is finding the

_____LESSONS_____

The following pages contain a few frames of a comic strip. To improve your ability to come up with *Lessons* take a moment and read the comic, then in the space provided, see if you can find a *Lesson* that can be learned from the comic.

It will only take you a few moments. Give it a try.

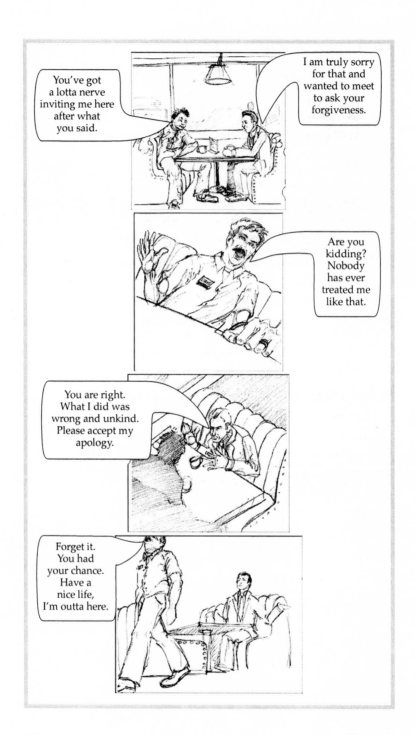

www.WaveStudyBible.com

Lessons

Write down what you can learn from this comic

Arguments can be difficult

Anger can cause us to be
unforgiving

Hurt can lead to unforgiveness

Asking for forgiveness doesn't
mean you will get it

Lessons

Arguments can be difficult

It takes two people to reconcile. Sometimes even if you do the right thing and ask for forgiveness the other person might not be willing to reconcile.

When someone is being hurtful to you, remember their opinion may change and they may ask for forgiveness at a later time.

It takes maturity to forgive when you have been wronged.

About the Comic Strip

Did you find something to learn from this comic?

This comic presents two people that are meeting to reconcile their differences. The offending person apologizes but the hurt person rejects the apology. The *Lesson* is not explicitly stated in the story (which is often the case in the Bible) so you have to come up with it.

If you see the apologizing person coming away from the experience feeling better for offering the apology, you could state the *Lesson* like this, "Even if your apology is rejected, it is good to do your part and apologize when you have offended someone."

If you see the apologizing person coming away from this experience amazed that his apology was not received, you could state the *Lesson* like this, "Even if you take all the right steps, it takes the cooperation of both people to reach a reconciliation."

As you study the Bible, when you have difficulty coming up with the *Lessons,* here are some things you can try.

Clues

The first step in finding a *Lesson* in a difficult passage is to pretend that you are a detective and back off the idea of getting a *Lesson* in one step. Rather, start look for clues that might lead you to a *Lesson*.

> 11. If you are stuck, try looking for
>
> _____CLUES_____

One possible clue in the comic is the genuine attitude of repentance from the one apologizing. He really sounds like he is sorry. But the other person does not respond by softening his attitude. These clues guide you to look at what can be learned when a genuine apology is rejected.

In the *Passage 1* homework there are also clues. Did you notice that each verse starts out with the phrase "By faith?" If you treat this as a clue, you might want to consider how Abraham was having to use faith. What assurances was he having to do without as he obeyed God's voice. It is sometimes God's desire for us to obey Him without all our questions answered.

When it is difficult to surface the *Lesson* in a single step, surface clues for a while and eventually a *Lesson* will emerge.

Points of View

The next thing to try is to look at the passage from different points of view. You may have viewed the comic strip from the point of view of the one apologizing as we did above. If a *Lesson* is not coming from that perspective, then think of the story from the other person's point of view.

---

12. Or try looking at the passage from

A DIFFERENT POINT OF VIEW

What *Lessons* could you learn from watching the other person? We can be trapped in anger if we refuse to forgive others. Forgiving benefits the victim the most because the aggressor still has to deal with his conscience.

The *Passage 1* homework can be viewed from the points of view of Abraham, Isaac and Jacob, Sarah, or God. From Isaac you can learn about how your world can be effected when God leads someone else in the family in a particular direction. From Sarah you can learn how God may allow barren times but He also can resolve them supernaturally.

When you have difficulty finding the Lesson, looking at the passage from different points of view will give you many more possibilities to consider.

Authors and Recipients

Keep in mind that every passage in the Bible is written by two authors and is written for two different recipients.

13. Or remember every passage has two

_____ AUTHORS _____

and two

_____ DIFFERENT RECIPIENTS _____

The two authors of any Bible passage are God and the human author. The human author of the passage might be someone like Paul, John, or Moses—whoever wrote that particular Bible book. The first of the two recipients are the ancient people, like the church at Ephesus or the Christians in Rome. We are the second recipient of every Bible passage.

So, as you look at the passage, consider the author/recipient combinations and ask yourself, "Why would the human author write this to the Galatians or why would God write this to us?" As you see the passage from these different vantage points, a *Lesson* will often present itself.

What is God Like?

If you can't find a *Lesson* using the other ideas, there is one thing you can always learn from any passage of scripture—you can always learn what kind of person God is.

14. Or you can always look at the passage and learn

WHAT KIND OF PERSON GOD IS

To say that God is a person or that He has a personality is not to say that God is a human being. He is not finite in any way. Rather, we are saying that God has a personality. There are things He likes and things He does not like. He holds some values as more important than other values. Some things move Him and other things do not.

As you look at your passage, notice how God acts, what He values, and what concerns Him. Then ask yourself, "What kind of person would act this way or value this kind of thing." Begin to build a mental picture of what kind of person God is.

Our goal is to know Him better so we can love and trust Him more. God tells Abraham to step out without giving him a lot of details. From this we can see that God is a strong leader. He is not anxiously hovering over His followers reminding them what they need to do next or what to be aware of. He gives a command and feels secure. We can learn about God's personality by watching how He behaves.

When you have difficulty coming up with a *Lesson* in your passage, give these ideas a try. Most of the time the *Lessons* are right under our nose. We just need to look at the passage from a different perspective to see them.

Assignment 3

For Your Mind

Study *Passage 2* in the *Abraham Workbook* on page 212.

If you have trouble surfacing the *Lessons*, try some of the tips discussed in this chapter. After you have worked on it, if you want some more ideas, take a look at the Appendix titled *Answers* on page 265.

For Your Heart

Set aside a few minutes each day to reflect on the seven questions described on page 41 and the three verses described on page 69 *(Ephesians 3:16-19, Matthew 12:30-31, and Luke 18:13)*. Ask God to help you grasp His love and respond to it.

At the request of people who have taken the course, these questions and verses have also been placed into a convenient reminder format in the Appendix titled *Reminder Card* on page 281. You can download a color version of this card from our web site, *http://www.WaveStudyBible.com*.

"Your mind
never stops working.
Incubation invites
illumination."

Dr. Howard Hendricks

"The point of life
is to get to know Jesus
in every situation."

Oswald Chambers

Chapter 4:
Walking Toward the Help

I [D] went to a 'secular' school for my Master's of Psychology degree. I think there was only one other Christian in the whole program. I remember raising my hand one day in class and commenting, "We are real big on the idea of boundaries in psychology. We teach our clients that it is OK to tell someone else that 'this' is OK with me, but 'this other thing' is not OK. And I agree that boundaries are important because without them there would be no right or wrong.

"But, I've noticed that psychology doesn't seem to like the idea that God might have boundaries! He has to be the big doormat in the sky. He has to accept whatever we justify in our own minds." Well, you could have heard a pin drop in the room after that.

God has boundaries. He wrote a whole book about them. They are reasonable and His help is available within them.

Running from the Help

There is a baffling tendency in all of us to turn and run from help. We are so sure we know a better way. But our actions so often separate us from the help we need.

In fact, this tendency is at the root of all sin. In its essence, sin is not wrong doing. Rather, <u>sin is independence from God</u>. Independent thinking says, "I'm not going to be anyone's disciple," "I'm my own boss," and "I do, what *I* want to do."

1. Sin is

   INDEPENDENCE FROM GOD

Most of us know non-Christians who behave better than many Christians. Going to heaven is not about behaving better than other people. Otherwise these well-behaved non-Christians would be going to heaven.

The reason non-Christians are not going to heaven is that they reject God's provision of forgiveness. They choose hell when they say, "I am my own boss. I don't need forgiveness." The Christian knows he is dependent on God's mercy and needs forgiveness.

2. Believers are dependent on

   GOD'S MERCY

God offers forgiveness and unconditional love within certain boundaries. He made the way. But independence from Him foils His efforts.

God's Pattern for Helping

In the last days of His ministry on earth, Jesus gave an object lesson during a meal that described how God was going to provide His help to us. Jesus wanted His disciples to understand what was going to happen the next few days. The object lesson is described in *Mark 14:22ff*.

> *Mark 14:22 And as they did eat, Jesus **took** bread, and **blessed**, and **brake** it, and **gave** to them, and said, Take, eat: this is my body. (KJV)*

As you may recognize, this was the last supper they had together and Jesus was describing how God was going to provide help for them. In the object lesson...

- Jesus took the bread,
- Jesus blessed the bread,
- Jesus broke the bread, and
- Jesus gave the bread.

---

3. Jesus...

_____TOOK_____ the bread

_____BLESSED_____ the bread

_____BROKE_____ the bread

_____GAVE_____ the bread

This pattern describes the way God worked with Jesus's life in that…

- God took Jesus,
- God blessed Jesus,
- God broke Jesus, and
- God gave Jesus.

4. God…

_____ _TOOK_ _____ Jesus

_____ _BLESSED_ _____ Jesus

_____ _BROKE_ _____ Jesus

_____ _GAVE_ _____ Jesus

This is the way God provides His help to us—He broke Jesus by placing our sin upon Him and gave Jesus over to receive the punishment that we deserve. This is also the way God works in our life and through our life to help others...

- God takes us,
- God blesses us,
- God breaks us, and
- God gives us.

5. God...

   _TAKES_____ us

   _BLESSES_____ us

   _BREAKS_____ us

   _GIVES_____ us

We like the "taking us" part and the "blessing us" part. But we cry foul at the "breaking us" part. *"He that loveth his life shall lose it." (John 12:25 KJV)* If we clutch at our life and say, "No, this is my life you can't have it," our life stays in our tight fist.

> John 12:24-28 *"I tell you the truth, unless a kernel of wheat falls to the ground and dies, it remains only a single seed. But if it dies, it produces many seeds. **The man who loves his life will lose it**, while the man who hates his life in this world will keep it for eternal life. Whoever serves me must follow me; and where I am, my servant also will be. My Father will honor the one who serves me. Now my heart is troubled, and what shall I say? 'Father, save me from this hour'? No, it was for this very reason I came to this hour. Father, glorify your name!" Then a voice came from heaven, "I have glorified it, and will glorify it again." (NIV)*

If we are not "broken" like that kernel of wheat falling to the ground and dying, our life remains a single seed, never leaving our clutches, never breaking away, never producing many seeds, and never being given to many.

Jesus wasn't crazy about the "breaking" process either. He said, "My heart is troubled." But He was willing to go through it.

I [D] remember watching the movie *Horse Whisperer* several years ago. If you didn't see the movie, it is about a young teenage girl who gets hit by a truck while riding her horse. The horse was badly injured and scared. The veterinarian and those who loved the horse kept trying to approach the horse to help him, but the horse kept bucking and rearing up and fighting the helpers because he was hurt and scared.

As I watched the movie, I realized I was like that horse. We had been going through a difficult time too and I found myself hurt, scared, and bucking around. But, just like the horse, I couldn't get the help I needed if I kept fighting the situation.

When you are struggling, fighting, and bucking, the thing that helps is to stop fighting, accept that you are in a difficult situation, and walk toward the help. Sometimes the help is confiding in a friend. Sometimes it is asking help from a pastor or professional. But it always includes walking toward God for help. When you walk toward God, you are agreeing to put His yoke on, as it says in *Matthew 11:28-30*, so you won't have to carry the whole burden.

> *Matthew 11:28-30* *"Come to me, all you who are weary and burdened, and I will give you rest.* **Take my yoke upon you** *and learn from me, for I am gentle and humble in heart, and you will find rest for your souls. For* **my yoke is easy and my burden is light.**" *(NIV)*

A yoke is a harness that helps two animals distribute the load between them. You will notice when God tells you to put His yoke on, you are still carrying some of the burden. You are in the yoke. But now you have help. You are not supposed to throw your burdens on God and try to forget them. You work as a team with God. Our burdens are not meant to be carried alone.

Jesus walked toward the task before Him. He was not bucking around. He wanted God to be glorified. Being fruitful implies carrying a burden. Picture a beautiful tree full of luscious fruit. It is carrying the burden of fruit it was meant to carry. It can feed and refresh many. But we can't bear fruit until we stop fighting and accept God's yoke.

God can redeem anything we give Him. He *works all things together for good to those who love Him. (Romans 8:28)* This is not a blank check. He is not promising to work all things together for good to those who hate Him and work against Him.

But, for those who love Him, He wants us to give Him our ugliest parts to fix. We have to be willing like the man in *Mark 3:1-6*.

> *Mark 3:1-6 Another time he went into the synagogue, and* **a man with a shriveled hand** *was there. Some of them were looking for a reason to accuse Jesus, so they watched him closely to see if he would heal him on the Sabbath. Jesus said to the man with the shriveled hand, "Stand up in front of everyone." Then Jesus asked them, "Which is lawful on the Sabbath: to do good or to do evil, to save life or to kill?" But they remained silent. He looked around at them in anger and, deeply distressed at their stubborn hearts, said to the man, "Stretch out your hand." He stretched it out, and his hand was completely restored. Then the Pharisees went out and began to plot with the Herodians how they might kill Jesus. (NIV)*

Can you imagine the man in *Mark 3:1-6* with the shriveled hand, being asked to stand in front of everyone and stretch out his most shameful part? This was a tough, judgemental crowd. But he was willing to do it and God redeemed his hand.

God can redeem whatever we give Him—even if the ugliness is of our own doing. It might take some time, but God can redeem it.

Don't clutch your independence. Be like a kernel of wheat and be willing to die to your own agenda. Walk toward God, by getting to know Him, so His love can compel you and your life can produce a harvest of seeds.

Notes

Desire Killer: Taking Offense

We have pointed out a couple of *Desire Killers*—*Deceitful Desires* and *Futile Thinking*—that can sabotage your desire to know God. The next *Desire Killer* to watch out for is found in *Mark 4* and *John 6*.

---

6. We have mentioned two *Desire Killers* to watch out for.

DECEITFUL DESIRES _____ and

FUTILE THINKING _____

The third *Desire Killer* is

TAKING OFFENSE _____

Mark 4:19-20 but the worries of this life, the deceitfulness of wealth and the desires for other things come in and choke the word, making it unfruitful. Others, like seed sown on good soil, hear the word, **accept it***, and produce a crop— thirty, sixty or even a hundred times what was sown. (NIV)*

John 6:53-56, 60-61, 66 Jesus said to them, "I tell you the truth, unless you eat the flesh of the Son of Man and drink his blood, you have no life in you. Whoever eats my flesh and drinks my blood has eternal life, and I will raise him up at the last day. For my flesh is real food and my blood is real drink. Whoever eats my flesh and drinks my blood remains in me, and I in him."

On hearing it, many of his disciples said, "This is a hard teaching. **Who can accept it?***" Aware that his disciples* *were grumbling about this, Jesus said to them, "**Does this offend you?**"*

From this time many of his disciples turned back and no longer followed him. (NIV)

The third *Desire Killer* that can stall your relationship with God is *Taking Offense*. We are vulnerable for *Taking Offense* because we don't have God's perspective. We don't have all the information. We should withhold judgment and take that thought captive.

In *John 6* the disciples heard Jesus say they needed to *"eat my flesh and drink my blood"* and went "eww... That sounds like cannibalism." They got on their moral high-horse pretty quickly, deciding they understood Jesus, and they concluded He was wrong. They were quick to *Take Offense*.

Jesus gave them a chance to clear up their misconception. He said, *"Does this offend you?"* But, they were too sure they understood and turned away, never to follow Him again.

We can *Take Offense* too. When evil triumphs and we don't understand what is going on, we can *Take Offense*. When we suffer loss and heartache, we can judge God and turn away. Sometimes we don't even admit that we have *Taken Offense*. We just subtly turn back and gradually leave God. But it is because we *Took Offense*.

The answer to this challenge is not complex but it requires some patience. When we feel tempted to *Take Offense*, we should remember that we don't have all the information.

Instead of deciding that we see all the issues clearly and quickly judging God, we should remind ourselves of His love, character, and trustworthiness. Then we should take our judgmental thought captive (as described on page 68).

7. When we feel tempted to *Take Offense* we should remember that we do not have

ALL THE INFORMATION and we should

TAKE OUR JUDGEMENTAL
THOUGHT CAPTIVE

Skill Time: Answering Your Questions

In this chapter's *Skill Time,* we describe what to do with questions that come up as you are studying the Bible.

Don't Focus on Your Questions

Normally in devotional Bible study it is best to put your focus on the parts of the passage that make sense to you rather than focusing on what you don't understand. The purpose of devotional Bible study is to feed yourself rather than to solve every problem you encounter.

8. Normally, in devotional Bible study, you shouldn't focus on

   THINGS you DONT UNDERSTAND

9. Rather, you should focus on

   THINGS THAT MAKES SENSE

Picture for a moment a cow walking out into a rich pasture full of luscious food in every direction. But over in the corner is a patch of ground where the grass is not growing very well. Now, it would not make sense for the cow to rush over to the barren part of the field and spend all its time trying to eat the grass that is barely growing when it is surrounded by such available food.

In a similar way, when you open a passage to study it, there are usually a number of things that make sense and some things you don't understand. Learn to focus on the things that make sense and so feed yourself from the richness of the field rather than spending all your time looking at problems and coming away from your study without nourishing your soul.

How to Answer Your Questions

Having said that, there are some times that it is worth the distraction to resolve questions that come up. For example, if you are preparing to teach a Bible passage to a group of people, you should probably answer some of the questions that occur in the passage so you can answer the group's questions. Or if you encounter a question that prevents you from understanding the rest of the passage, that might be a good question to answer for yourself.

Once you have a question, it is sometimes unclear how you should go about answering it. Consider how children's questions are answered.

If you are a parent, or have been around children, you probably have had to answer a lot of questions. Many of the questions are on topics familiar to you, but some of them are on unfamiliar topics. Yet they still want an answer. So you probably do your best to piece together a likely answer.

For example, suppose a circus has come to town and you take a small child to watch the circus parade down the street. As you watch, a plate spinner goes by and a child asks how they do that. You may have to think for a minute or two. Then you might speculate that there is probably a groove in the bottom of the plate that the stick fits into. Or perhaps the plates stay stable because of the high speed at which they are spinning. As long as the plate is spun quickly and the stick remains in the middle, it works. One way or the other, you give your best guess and surprisingly, your best guess is often quite close.

Steps

When you have a Bible study question you want to answer, use the following steps.

Pray for Wisdom

It is surprising how often the answer to our question is right before our eyes in plain view but we don't see it. Pause, take some time. Ask God to open your eyes and help you see. He loves to give us wisdom *(James 1:5)* and He does open our eyes.

10. But, when you need to answer a question, *Step 1:* is to

PRAY FOR WISDOM

List All Possible Answers

Take a look at your question, take a look at the passage, and imagine as many answers as you can. The answers do not need to be perfectly supportable, they just need to be potential statements that would answer your question. If you work with it, you can usually come up with at least two or three possible answers.

11. *Step 2:* List all the

POSSIBLE ANSWERS

If you can't think of any possibilities, then imagine the most persistent child you know is asking the question. This child will not take "I don't know" for an answer. Whatever you would tell that child is what you should write down.

This is a creative step. Take the leash off your mind and let it run freely and write down what you come up with.

Write Out the Support for Each Answer

Look at the first answer, then look at the passage and write down all the reasons that would support this being the answer to your question. Then do the same thing for each of the other possible answers.

12. *Step 3:* Write out the support for

EACH POSSIBLE ANSWER

At this point you are making an argument for each answer. Be as unbiased as you can. Surface everything you can see or think of that supports the answer.

Choose the Best Answer Based on the Support

Now sit back and survey the possible answers and their support. You are judge and jury. The Holy Spirit is opening your eyes. Decide for yourself, which answer has the greatest chance of being correct based on the strength of its support. That is the answer to your question.

13. *Step 4:* Choose the best answer based on

THE STRENGTH OF ITS SUPPORT

Check an Authority

Once you have surfaced and weighed the evidence and have an opinion of your own, it is a good time to compare your opinion with the opinion of an authority or two.

14. *Step 5:* Check an

_____AUTHORITY_____

You might use an online resource or go to a Christian bookstore and look for commentaries that cover your passage to see if they address your question. You might ask a pastor, or other church leader whose opinion you trust, what their answer would be to your question and why they favor that answer.

As you check with these authorities, if they cover your question and suggest an answer, be careful what you do with the answer. Do not discard your answer and adopt the authority's answer because the authority may have studied more than you.

Rather, go back to your list of possible answers and support for each answer and add the new information contributed by the authority. Now sit back and decide which answer seems right based on the strength of its support.

Remember, when you meet the Lord in heaven, He is not going to ask you what your pastor thinks. He is going to ask you what *you* think. Go with the answer that makes the most sense to *you*.

Can Anyone Do This?

When it comes to answering your own questions, some people worry they are not smart enough. In devotional Bible study, smartness is not the issue. Let me illustrate.

There was a popular eschatological scholar who went from town to town giving lectures on the end time events described in the Bible. He made a living untangling the complex imagery described in the books of Ezekiel, Daniel, and Revelation and explaining them to church congregations.

He arrived at a certain city to hold a week long conference on end time prophecy. During the week he had an appointment to meet someone at a local High School. As he walked through the school to find his appointment location, he passed by an open door that caught his attention. He had some time, so he stepped into the doorway to investigate.

He found himself in a large gymnasium. The gymnasium was empty except for an old humble janitor sitting on a bleacher on the other side of the room. What caught the conference speaker's attention was what the janitor had in his lap. It looked like he had a Bible.

The conference speaker crossed the room and came to the janitor and sat down. As he did, he was interested to notice the man was reading from the book of Revelation.

The speaker said to him, "I notice you are reading the book of Revelation. Do you understand what you are reading?" The elderly janitor replied, "Well, yes sir, I think I do." Intrigued, the scholar asked, "So tell me, what does it mean?" The janitor thought for a second then replied, "God wins in the end."

You don't have to be smart to understand the Bible. What God wants you to understand is simple enough for a child to understand *(Matthew 19:14).*

The Rest of the Answers?

Another worry that some people have about devotional Bible study, is how they will ever get the bulk of their questions answered if they don't focus on the things they don't understand. That is best explained by the following true illustration.

An experiment was conducted in a college level pottery class. The students were split into two groups. One group was told it would be graded solely on *how many* pots they made. The more they made, the higher their grade, regardless of the quality of the pots. The other group was told it would be graded solely on the *quality* of the pots it made.

At the end of the course the best pots from both groups were compared. Can you guess which group produced the highest quality pots? Logically you would expect the group that was graded on the quality of their pots to have the highest quality pots. However, the group that was graded on *how many* pots they made, was found to have the highest quality pots.

Practice makes perfect. The more you study the Bible, the more you come across the answers to your questions. Also, the more you grow, the fewer questions you will need answered and the more things you will trust God about. The more you study the Bible and grow in your walk with the Lord, the more your questions will be resolved.

Assignment 4

For Your Mind

Study *Passage 3* and read the commentary that follows in the *Abraham Workbook* on page 218.

If you come across something in the passage that intrigues you, write it out as a question and go through the five steps of answering your own questions on page 100.

For Your Heart

To change your desires and thinking, keep praying the verses on the reminder card on page 283.

"Faith in God's character is the heroic effort of life. Have reckless confidence in God."

Oswald Chambers

Chapter 5:
Removing Thorns

When an elephant is very young, one end of a rope is tied around one of its feet and the other is tied to a stake in the ground. The elephant is not big enough or strong enough to dislodge the stake so, before long, it stops trying.

After the elephant grows up, the stake is no longer needed. All they have to do is tie one end of a rope around the elephant's foot, leaving the other end free, and the elephant will not attempt to wander off. At an early age the elephant learned that it was impossible to walk away when the rope was tied to its foot, so there is no need to try it again.

The experiences you have when you are young and the way you chose to respond to those experiences become a collection of learned patterns that follow you throughout life. They are lessons you have learned and conclusions you have made about yourself and the world around you.

Since these patterns were learned at an early age they have been integrated into your collection of automatic reactions and you seldom, if ever, question them.

In most cases the patterns are helpful. Lessons you learned as a child like "Don't run into a street when a car is coming," "Don't touch a hot stove," "Hard work pays off," and "Honesty is the best policy" provide healthy automatic patterns for adult behavior.

But some patterns you learned were only appropriate when you were a small child under some difficult experience like "Stay clear of dad, he is always in a bad mood," "Make sure you are no trouble to anyone so you don't make mom feel worse," or "My parents don't come through for me so I won't count on people." Even though you don't need these patterns after you grow up, they have been integrated into your automatic reactions and you continue to live by them. These inappropriate patterns can cause you to behave in ways that may not make sense to your current situation.

This can be especially true when you deal with God. God the Father treats us like family *(Galatians 4:6-7)*, Jesus treats us like family *(Matthew 12:50)*, and our natural response back to God is a family response. That is when our learned *Family of Origin* patterns kick in. Your *Family of Origin* is the family you grew up in. Most of the time, the patterns you respond with are appropriate and make sense to apply toward God.

1. Your *Family of Origin* is the family

<u>I GREW UP IN</u>

But when our learned patterns are not appropriate to apply toward God, they become *Family of Origin Issues* and need to be updated.

Family of Origin Issues

There are two kinds of experiences in your *Family of Origin* that can hinder your walk with God.

The first is if you trusted a significant adult in your past and then got burned. If that is the background you bring to the Christian life, it may be harder for you to trust God.

Now, some people are hesitant to think about their *Family Of Origin Issues (FOOI pronounced FOO eee)*. They think if they do so, they are being disloyal to their parents. But, if you are willing to face unfinished business that is still affecting you today, you will end up able to love your parents more, not less. You will no longer be a "victim." of automatic reactions.

Parents are responsible for taking care of their children from birth until 18 years of age. Once you turn 18, *you* are responsible to take over the care of yourself, not your parents.

2. It is your parent's job to meet your needs from birth to

   18 YEAR OF AGE

3. After that, meeting your needs is

   MY RESPONSIBILITY

If you are a parent and you unwittingly did something that hurt your child, would you want them to stand before God and say "my parents damaged me a bit so I wasn't able to serve You very much?" Or would you want them to face the problem, take responsibility and fix it so they could be good stewards of the life God has given them?

If you face your unfinished business, you are not being disloyal, you are being responsible. We are more familiar with how *FOOI* can hinder our relationships, but *Mark 4:7* may suggest how *FOOI* can hinder us spiritually.

> Mark 4:7 *Other seed fell among* **thorns**, *which grew up and choked the plants, so that they did not bear grain. (NIV)*

I [D] think the "thorns" that choked out the fruitfulness of the plants in *Mark 4:7* could be unfinished business from past *FOOI*. These patterns are automatic and can significantly hinder your ability to give yourself wholeheartedly to our heavenly Father.

Are there any issues, related to growing up, that may be choking out your fruitfulness? For instance, if one of your parents was unavailable emotionally, you might be tempted to think God is unavailable to you as well.

The second way you might have experienced *FOOI* is if you encountered unique circumstances like the loss of a parent for example. That is how I experienced *FOOI*. My father died unexpectedly when I was 3 years old. Because of that, I found that total surrender to the Lord was harder because I feared something catastrophic might happen. I didn't realize that I was living my adult life from a three year old's mind-set. My three year old mind-set said that life "happens" to you. You have no power or options. It is all "God's sovereignty" and no "man's responsibility." Unlike most adults who take responsibility and make use of their resources, I had a three year old's powerless mind-set. This made me more worried about surrendering to God because I felt powerless to deal with what He might allow.

Family Of Origin Issues and Bible Study

Whatever *FOOI* you may have picked up along the way follows you into every area of your Christian life. *FOOI* can even contaminate how you interpret the Bible.

4. *FOOI* effects how you interpret

_THE BIBLE_____

For example, when you read *Romans 3:23* you could have one of a few different responses.

> *Romans 3:23 for **all have sinned** and fall short of the glory of God. (NIV)*

In a balanced response you might be sobered. You would figure that we all might fall short, but there is some relief in the fact that we are all in the same boat. It would also be a relief to learn that God is not in the boat. He is greater than us.

But a *FOOI* response might say, "God is impossible to please just like my dad (or mom). They were impossible to please. I always fell short of their requirements no matter what. God might have paid for my sins, but I am convinced that He is not OK with me."

Be careful not to put your *FOOI* on God. If you could never please a parent, that parent was not OK.

I heard of a teenage boy who could never please his father. The boy was excited when he got straight A's on his report card. He thought to himself, "Now dad will have to be pleased." But when he showed the report card to his father, his father slammed his fist onto the table and said, "I knew you could get all A's. You have been holding out on me. Why haven't you been doing this all along?"

If you had a parent who could never be pleased, there was something wrong in their life. Don't put your parent's face on God and you will get much more from your Bible study.

---

5. God does not have your parent's

   _____FACE_____

Get to Know God

The antidote for much of *FOOI* is to get to know God. He is your new parent and is very reasonable and kind. The better you know Him and replace old patterns with patterns consistent with what God is like, the less your *FOOI* will contaminate your present life.

6. The antidote for much of *FOOI* is to

   <u>GET TO KNOW GOD</u>

One helpful way to get to know God is to start compiling a list that describes what God is like. As you study a passage and learn a new trait of God's, add it to your list and begin to get a profile of your new parent. Here are some traits to get you started.

- God is slow to anger
  (Exodus 34:6)

- God's mercies are new every morning
  (Lamentations 3:23)

- God is rich in kindness
  (Exodus 34:6)

- God is Holy
  (1 Samuel 2:2, Isaiah 6:3)

- God always does what is right
  (Genesis 18:25)

- God is perfect
  (Deuteronomy 32:4)

- God is not needy
  (Acts 17:25)

- God is love
  (1 John 4:8)

- God never sins when He is angry
  (Deuteronomy 32:4)

- God made a way for me to be forgiven
  (John 3:16)

- God has my best interest in mind
  (Luke 11:13)

Identify How God Differs From Your Parents

As you get a profile of what God is like, pay particular attention to how He differs from your parents. You might be surprised to learn what "delights" God in *Jeremiah 9:24*.

> *Jeremiah 9:24* "*Boast in this… that he understands and* **knows Me**, *that I am the Lord who exercises kindness, justice, and righteousness on earth, for in these I delight.*" *(NIV)*

In *Jeremiah 9:24* God asserts that He wants us to understand and know the real Him. He doesn't want us to mistake Him for some flawed composite of our parents.

7. God wants us to know Him, not a flawed composite

   OUR PARENTS.

It is OK for a seven year old to think God is like his parents. It is not so appropriate for an adult to think God is like his earthly parents. God doesn't have a hair trigger temper or mean streak, or whatever flaw may have characterized your parents.

When you are having trouble trusting God, see if your difficulty might be connected to *FOOI*. Get quiet and notice more carefully if your response to God is fear, anger, sadness, or something else. See if your response feels "old" from your past. Do you remember frequently feeling like this in response to a parent?

As you think about your response, start thinking about how God differs from your parents. If you are worried that God is explosive because you had an explosive Dad, start listing how God is different: He is slow to anger, His mercies are new every morning, He made the way for you to be forgiven.

Sometimes we have learned responses to life situations from the past. For example, if things are going well yet you are having trouble enjoying it, that could be a learned response. Who did you learn it from?

Maybe mom was volatile and moody and you couldn't trust her "good mood" because you knew her good mood could turn on a dime and you needed to be ready to duck. That is a learned response and it can easily contaminate your relationship with God.

When you are trying to trust God, but feel troubled because of *FOOI*, it helps to…

- Get quiet and pray for wisdom

- Write down what your response to God is—fear, sadness, anger,…?

- Look for the source of your response—is it learned from a parent, is it similar to how you responded to a parent?

- Write down how God differs from your parent concerning this issue.

These steps help you surface the *FOOI* pattern that is distracting you and it helps you learn something about God that can give you relief from the difficult life experience.

If you had difficult parents, *Psalm 27:10* says that God is kind and will receive you. God is not like our flawed parents. He must get weary of the accusation.

> *Psalm 27:10 Though my father and mother forsake me, **the Lord will receive me.** (NIV)*

If you find yourself struggling with the idea of authority and suspect that *FOOI* may be involved, consider this: Ice cream is delicious unless it is jammed down your throat. But ice cream is still delicious. The problem is not with the ice cream but with the manner in which it was served.

If you had difficult parents and they jammed "authority" down your throat, the problem is not with authority, but with how it was served. God won't jam it down your throat. He is kind.

Start tuning in to your reactions as you study the Bible and serve God. When you detect a *FOOI* pattern at work, surface what is going on and distinguish how God differs from the significant authorities of the past.

Skill Time: Transformation by Imitation

This chapter's *Skill Time* focuses on a way to help you experience the *Lessons* you surface in Bible study.

The idea involves the simplest form of learning—*Imitation*. Children use it to learn to speak, apprentices use it to learn their trade, and athletes use it to learn their skill.

Let me introduce *Imitation* by describing an experience I had some years back.

Learning by Imitation

I [N] was invited to perform in a Master Class for the classical guitar. Pepe Romero was the teacher (cf. *www.peperomero.com*). Pepe played in a very successful quartet with his father and two brothers and they are known as Spain's Royal Family of the Spanish Guitar.

What intrigued me was that all of the sons in the family ended up doing what their father did. So I asked Pepe how his father managed to encourage all his boys to play the classical guitar. Pepe answered, "I don't know. He must have been pretty sneaky, because I was never told to practice." "But," he continued, "we didn't have a TV and there were always guitars lying around the house. And every morning I would hear my father practicing."

Pepe's father was the only guitar teacher Pepe had, but he only remembers having two or three guitar lessons from his father. Pepe's main instruction did not come from guitar lessons, it came from imitating his father. When his father would practice, Pepe would watch him play, then go and try to do it himself.

Imitation is the simplest and most natural way for any of us to learn. It transcends words. You just watch somebody doing something then go and try it yourself.

Transformation is Imitation Over Time

We already know that *Transformation* comes from renewing our mind (cf. page 66). In *2 Corinthians 3:18*, the Bible explains mind renewing further by describing what we are to be thinking about.

> *2 Corinthians 3:18 But we all, with unveiled face, **beholding** as in a mirror the glory of the Lord, **are being transformed** into the same image from glory to glory, just as from the Lord, the Spirit. (NASB)*

We are to be thinking about the Lord. That gives us a mental image of what He is like—what He values, how He acts, what moves Him, what brings Him joy, and what brings Him sadness.

As we experience time focusing on God, something special happens. Whenever we focus on a person for a period of time, we start becoming like them. This is called the process of *Imitation*.

You become like the person you watch.

8. Transformation is *Imitation*

   _____

9. You become like the person you

   _____

Our spiritual *Transformation* is a mental process in which we watch the Lord and *Imitate* Him over time. As you compile your list of what God is like, take some time in prayer to behold Him and enjoy the experience of being with Him. The more we see the Lord, the more we are *Transformed* into His image.

Give it a Try

This simple tool can help you experience the *Lessons* you surface in Bible study.

To give it a try, pick a *Lesson* from one of your recent Bible studies. Then pretend for a minute that you suddenly had whatever was needed so you were able to do that *Lesson* with absolutely no difficulty. With this new ability, the *Lesson* makes total sense to you and seems easy.

For instance, what if you were doing the *Lesson*, "We can have faith in God's promises when there is no outward reason to have hope." You would visualize yourself going through a typical day with this new ability. Watch how you react to things, how you feel, and what decisions you make when you have this ability to believe God's promises.

Is anything different from what usually happens during a typical day? As you picture yourself going through your day, do you feel different? Do you react differently? Do you value things differently? Enjoy the picture for a while.

What is interesting about this exercise is the picture you visualize for yourself is surprisingly realistic. That is why you can learn from it. You might guess that you would act rigidly and not in touch with things around you in this picture. But you are picturing yourself with a very natural new ability and so the picture you visualize is surprisingly natural.

If you can visualize yourself successfully doing *Lessons* from your Bible study, God can use *Imitation* to help you gradually incorporate the *Lessons* into your daily life.

Assignment 5

For Your Mind

Study *Passage 4* in the *Abraham Workbook* on page 224.

Then pick one of the *Lessons* and picture yourself able to do that *Lesson* perfectly. Picture yourself going through a normal day with this new ability and take note of any differences in what you feel or do.

For Your Heart

To change your desires and thinking, keep praying the verses on the reminder card on page 283. Notice your hesitations and see if any of them are linked to *Family Of Origin Issues*.

Nurture your desire. The stronger it gets, the harder it is to cover up.

"The expression of
Christian character
is not doing good,
but God-likeness."

Oswald Chambers

"Don't put
your parent's face
on God."

The Authors

Chapter 6:
Stretching Your Comfort Zone

Surfing was very popular when I [N] was growing up in Southern California so I gave it a try. Wow, I can still see the first time a wave lifted me, I stood on the board, navigated to the shoulder of the wave and had my first long ride. It was exhilarating, it was refreshing, and it was fun.

But surfing takes place in a very small area of the wave. Surfing in a crowded area is much like driving on the freeway during rush hour. Everyone is tightly packed together, taking risks, and operating on a system of unwritten rules that go far beyond the motor vehicle code. Invariably at crowded surfing spots tempers would flare and fights would break out.

I loved surfing but as a young kid and an *Introvert*, I didn't want anything to do with the fights. So, I switched surfing styles from stand-up surfing to spooning (a style like boogie boarding). This provided a natural separation between me and the fighting element so I could surf within my comfort zone. The only problem was that spooning was not as fun as stand-up surfing.

As an adult, I spent 15 years out of state. When I returned to Southern California I was eager to get back into surfing. As I reoriented myself, I had to decide if I was going to continue spooning or go back to stand-up surfing. I was not a kid any more and the reasons I had avoided stand-up surfing seemed silly, so I got a surfboard and went for it.

Eventually the thing I dreaded happened—my board and a hot head's board touched and I found myself in an unavoidable fight in the water. Fortunately, I got the upper hand and was able to keep him at bay. But I hated the whole intimidation atmosphere where people threaten to kill you over a bumped board.

As I drove home from the beach that day I faced a decision. How badly did I want to surf? Was I willing to go beyond my comfort zone and take on these kinds of people or not? It took a long time for me to sort this out and I came close to giving up surfing and taking up another kind of exercise.

But in the end I decided, as an adult, I could make choices that improved my situation, and I could go after what I really wanted. It just might be uncomfortable for a while.

So, I decided to improve my situation. I surfed at less crowded spots and honed my surfing skills. Then I went to more crowded spots and would sit in the midst of the lineup watching others position for the waves and take or yield right-of-way. As I watched, I discovered a whole network of unspoken rules that went way beyond the basic right-of-way rules in surfing. Eventually, I got to the place where I was comfortable surfing in crowded areas and could successfully negotiate the hotheads.

It is never easy to step out of your comfort zone. But, as an adult, you are able to make decisions that improve your situation and help you skillfully negotiate the discomfort until you reach the goal.

Biblical Comfort Zone Examples

All the great people of the Bible faced fears. They all had to move out of their comfort zone: Abraham, Joseph, Jacob, Samuel, Moses, Daniel, David, Paul, and Peter. But there are two Bible characters that did not move out of their comfort zone. And though their lives started out promising, they ended sadly.

The first of these is Solomon. He was the second son of David and Bathsheba. God does not look at pedigree and did not exclude Solomon from His blessing because of his parent's sin. Solomon asked for wisdom and God gave it to him, but he didn't always use it.

You know how sometimes you know the right thing to do, but you choose to do otherwise? Solomon focused his life on the pursuit of pleasure. He took in seven hundred wives and three hundred concubines and they brought their foreign gods with them. This became a problem for Solomon. His pursuit of pleasure got him off course. Solomon spent his life chasing after the *Deceitful Desires* of sex, money, and things. Then, at the end of his life he threw up his hands and said of his efforts, *"all is vanity and striving after wind."* (Ecclesiastes 1:14 NASB) He misspent his life trying to hold onto comfort and pleasure instead of being willing to leave his comfort zone.

1. Solomon misspent his life trying to hold on to

_____ and

_____

The other Bible character that did not step out of his comfort zone was Saul. Saul was the most handsome man in Israel and God picked him to be their king. Saul was reluctant at first, but God transformed him for the task.

Then, instead of staying humble and obedient to accomplish what God had in mind, he became headstrong and disobedient. When he heard God planned to give his throne to David, he did not humble himself to accept God's consequences, but became obsessed and paranoid trying to protect his power. He spent his time and effort running around the country trying to kill David instead of asking

God to protect his throne. He was not willing to leave his comfort zone and trust God with his life.

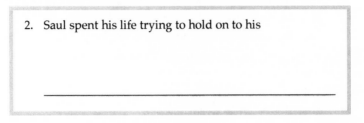

2. Saul spent his life trying to hold on to his

_____

Our job is to be a good steward of the life God gives us and be willing to step out of our comfort zone when called upon.

Introverts and Extroverts

Responding to God

Our *FOOI* can make it harder for us to obey God's word and step out of our comfort zone. For example, in *1 John 1:9* God challenges us that if we step out of our comfort zone (confess our sins), we will receive forgiveness. This verse is pretty straightforward but your background may slant how you respond to it.

> *1 John 1:9* **If we confess** our sins, He is faithful and just and **will forgive** us our sins and purify us from all unrighteousness. (NIV)

If you were never held accountable growing up, you will tend to blame others for your mistakes. This is called *Projection*. You *Project* blame onto others. You say, "My problems are someone else's fault."

If this is your tendency, when you read this verse you probably have trouble thinking of anything to confess because everything is someone else's fault. You push responsibility off yourself and onto others so you don't think the verse applies to you much.

3. *Extroverts* tend to

_____

On the other hand, when you were growing up, if you believed most things were your fault, you learn to *Introject*, or take on too much responsibility. You blame yourself inappropriately. This person says, "If the people around me are angry or sad, it is probably my fault."

People that approach life from this point of view worry they are really forgiven. When they come to *1 John 1:9* they have trouble believing that they have confessed well enough. Saying you are sorry to a critical parent doesn't usually help much.

4. *Introverts* tend to

_____

But *1 John 1:9* is very simple and straightforward. We confess, He is faithful and just to forgive. We complicate it with *FOOI*. It does not say if we confess with just the right tone and expression on our face, He will forgive. We just have to confess. He is faithful to forgive.

A balanced person takes responsibility for their sin, takes God at His word, and confesses. That's it.

5. A balanced person responds to the verse by taking

_____ for their sin, taking God at His

_____ and

_____

Know Your Tendency

I [D] have noticed in my private practice that *Introverts* tend to *Introject*. They tend to accept too much responsibility for a problem. *Extroverts* tend to *Project*. They don't accept enough responsibility. That's why *Extroverts* feel good most of the time—nothing is ever their fault.

Now there are balanced *Introverts* and balanced *Extroverts* who accept responsibility for their part and no more. It is helpful to notice your tendency so you can correct for it.

Dr. Noel is an *Introvert* and tends to *Introject*. I'm more of an *Extrovert* and tend to *Project*. When we were first married I inadvertently got away with murder. I *Projected* and assigned the blame for things and he *Introjected* and accepted it! Then after a few years he wised up and figured it couldn't always be all his fault. Now it is better for both of us. It is better for me to be accountable for my part so I can grow, and it is better for him not to be shouldering all the blame.

Making Someone Mad?

Let me say a word to those of you who *Introject* and accept too much responsibility. In our culture it is common to hear the phrase, "You make me so mad." That is an overstatement. You don't have the power to make anyone mad without their permission.

When our kids were in school, one of their teachers always got under my skin. Every time I was around him, I found myself getting angry. Then one day I had too much going on to be reacting to him, so I decided to be apathetic about his behavior that day. That was the day I first realized that he didn't have the power to make me angry. His behavior was irritating, but I did not have to be irritated. It wasn't worth the effort.

Have you ever tried to cheer up someone who doesn't want to be cheered up? Has anyone tried to cheer you up when you weren't done being angry or sad? You are not going to be cheered up until you decide you are ready.

We don't have power to control another person's emotions. Some people have allowed themselves to become very reactive to everyone around them, but they are choosing to be reactive. They could learn to be more apathetic to some of the stimulus around them.

You are not responsible for someone else's anger. You are responsible for your own behavior.

6. You do not have the power to make someone

_____

Humility is Answer for Both

Humility is the answer for both the *Introvert* and the *Extrovert*. If you *Introject* and accept too much blame, you need to know your limits. Humble yourself and realize you are not as powerful as you think. You can not control the people around you.

If you *Project* and don't accept enough blame, you need to humble yourself and take responsibility for your sins. You are not perfect.

---

7. The answer for both the *Introvert* and the *Extravert* is

_____

Get to Know God

The best way to keep your *FOOI* from distorting your experience with God is to get to know God.

For example, if you find you are having trouble trusting God, see if you are reacting to Him like you reacted to one of your parents. If so, contrast what that parent is like against what God is like. The better you know God, the better you will neutralize your *FOOI*. He is certainly different than your parents. Keep adding to your list of what God is like (see page 112).

In *Psalm 34:18-19* God reminds us how strong and compassionate He is. He delivers us from all our troubles.

> *Psalm 34:18-19 The Lord is **close** to the brokenhearted and **saves** those who are crushed in spirit. A righteous man may have many troubles, but the Lord **delivers** him from them **all**; (NIV)*

8. God is strong and

_____

Dr. Tony Evans said when he was a boy, his parents got him a punching bag that sat on the floor and would rock back and forth as he punched on it. One day he punched it so hard it ricocheted around the room, bouncing off the walls, boom, boom, boom, until it finally righted itself on the floor and began to sway back and forth, bing, bing, bing—bink!

He said that is what life can seem like at times. We are ricocheting off the walls of life, bouncing around, but God will right us. We will go boom, boom, boom, bing, bing, bing—bink! He delivers us from all our troubles. When you need to move beyond your comfort zone it is good to know that God is right there promising to deliver you.

Getting to know God will smooth out your *FOOI* and it will provide true comfort that is absent from *Deceitful Desires*. According to *2 Corinthians 1:3-4*, God is the Father of compassion and the God of all comfort.

> *2 Corinthians 1:3-4 Praise be to the God and Father of our Lord Jesus Christ, the **Father of compassion** and the **God of all comfort**, who comforts us in all our troubles, so that we can comfort those in any trouble with the comfort we ourselves have received from God. (NIV)*

9. God is the Father of compassion and the God of all

_____

Are we looking to God for comfort? He stands ready to give it to us. Or are we looking to something else for comfort: a new gadget or car, the mall, food, TV, work, or leisure?

It took us awhile to select what we turn to for comfort. We didn't just instantly know the best foods to turn to for comfort, or the best videos or TV shows to watch to cheer us up. We figured that out by experimenting. We need to do the same thing when turning to God for comfort. It might take us awhile to figure out how to read the Bible and ask God specifically for comfort.

As you practice asking God for comfort, take note of your attitude when asking. Do you have a chip on your shoulder and a resistance to being "cheered up?" If we aren't ready to be cheered up, we won't allow God to comfort us.

10. Looking to God for comfort will take

_____

Skill Time: Finding the Time

Now it is time to discuss how to pick a time for your personal time with God. If you already have a time that works well for you, the chances are good that at some point, your life circumstances will change and you will need to adjust your time slot. The following ideas will help any time you need to select a time slot for your personal time with God.

The Problem

Whenever we attempt to add a regular activity to our schedule there appears to be no room for it. We have already stretched our schedules to meet the demands of our modern lives.

It looks like our schedules are completely unchangeable. We have worked so hard to get our schedules to work as poorly as they do, we don't want to risk making things worse.

> 11. *The Problem:* It looks like our schedules are
>
> _____

This kind of thinking is a problem because when you think like this you tend to rule out possible time slots without giving the necessary thought to what might be possible.

Some people address this problem by suggesting you put your time with God anywhere in your schedule, then make that time work by raw dedication, determination, and perseverance. Others focus on the amount of time and suggest ways of trimming the time down so far that your time with God fits into a crack in your schedule that is hardly noticeable.

For most people, neither of these approaches help their time with God compete effectively with the demands of their busy life. The steps below do a better job of putting your time with God in a place to succeed.

Steps

Select the Best Time of Day

Temporarily wipe your schedule completely clean. Pretend, for a minute, that you have no time commitments whatsoever.

Now, focus on the kind of activity you would like to do in your time with God and identify what kind of energy it requires. Does it require high energy, meditative energy, peacefulness, or just an alert task orientation?

Once you have identified what kind of energy you would like for your time with God, think through when that kind of energy is available to you. Is that kind of energy most likely available at noon time, late at night, or in the morning? Remember you have wiped your schedule clean. Your only concern here is to discover when you have the kind of energy you need to have your time with God.

12. *Step 1:*

_____ and select the best

_____

Select the Frequency that Matches Your Desire

After you have identified the ideal time of day for your time with God, decide how much time each session should be and how many sessions to have each week.

To answer this question, you must consult the *Desire* you have been surfacing. You should select an amount of time that is enough to challenge you, but not too much to overwhelm your current *Desire*.

For some people that might be 2 or 3 times per week for 15 minutes each. The amount of time varies widely between individuals. The stronger your *Desire*, the more it can support.

Don't make the mistake of trying to be immediately perfect. People frequently make this mistake when trying to add exercise to their schedule. They buy a gym membership and decide they will come every day for 1 hour. Most burn out within a month because they overshoot their desire. Be honest with yourself. Find where your desire level is and start there. It will grow.

13. *Step 2:* Select the frequency that matches your

_____

Wrap Your Life Around It

Once you decide on the best time slots, wrap your whole life around it.

Don't be fooled into assuming it is impossible to clear your ideal time slot. You are an adult. You can make decisions that change things. You have power and creativity.

It might mean you have to go to bed earlier and record TV shows for later viewing, or just stop watching some TV shows. It might mean you change how you eat lunch so you have time at lunch time. It might mean you go into work a bit later in the morning.

14. *Step 3:* Wrap your life

_____

Example

I [N] went through these steps and decided I wanted my time with God in the morning, but after I had my shower and breakfast so I would be awake.

So, I went to bed earlier, got up earlier, and had my time with God after I got ready for work. But the whole time I kept thinking about all the cars that were piling onto the freeway ahead of me and how slow rush hour would be when I got there.

Then I decided I would leave the house early, get to work early, avoid rush hour, and have my time with God in my office before others got there. Well, I avoided rush hour all right, but I just couldn't feel right having my time with God in my office. After all, I was at work and I should be working.

At this point I had tried two things and they didn't work. Should I give up? No, I am an adult. Adults have the power to make decisions and changes that improve their situation. So I kept experimenting.

If I was an *Extrovert*, my next step would be to figure out a way to have my time with God in a fast food place like McDonald's. I could stay as long as I needed and I could write out the prayer portion of my time with God.

But, as an *Introvert*, I ended up selling my beloved VW bug and bought a used van which I converted into a surf van. I drove it to work early in the morning, got comfortable with pillows in the back and had my time with God alone in the van before work. I got there before rush hour so avoided the traffic and had my own environment to enjoy my time with God. The bonus was that I now had a way to surf at lunch time since I could carry my surfboard in the van and change in the back.

If you dare to think ideally, you can get your life to line up with your true values.

Assignment 6

For Your Mind

Study *Passage 5* in the *Abraham Workbook* on page 232.

Take a moment, wipe your schedule clean, and figure out what would be the very best time slot for your time with God. Then make a first attempt at wrapping your life around it.

For Your Heart

To change your desires and thinking, keep meditating on the six questions and praying the three verses on page 282. The questions can quietly orient your thinking and surface your desire. Praying the three verses back to God helps you value God's perspective. If you notice resistance when you think about following God wholeheartedly, look to see if you could be relating to God like you related to one of your parents.

Add to your list of what God is like. What moves Him? What makes Him sing or be joyful, grieved or angry? What does He care about?

Look for at least one opportunity to go to God for comfort instead of following whatever pattern is normal for you. Then as you study the Bible assignment, notice if you have any resistance (anger, fear, sadness) to any *Lesson* that might nudge you beyond your comfort zone. Consider if the resistance could be related to *FOOI* or to an *Introvert / Extrovert* tendency.

"Don't focus
on the mountain."

Bill Hybels

Chapter 7:
Aligning Your Prayers

I saw fear in her eyes. It was the week after High School graduation and I [N] was expecting to see relief and celebration. But
our oldest daughter was showing signs of apprehension about
her upcoming entrance into college.

Even though she had been a good student in High School, the
transition to college was full of uncertainty. Would she know
what classes to take? Would she be successful? So many things
would be on her shoulders.

As I thought about her situation, I came up with an activity that
would channel some of that energy into a task that might help
her confidence. I asked her to get her college catalog and we
found the place that discussed her major. Then I said, "Everything you need to know about graduating from college is described in these pages. I want you to read them and be able to
explain the requirements for graduation. I will expect you to
know things like the meaning of 'General Education' units. In
one week I will quiz you."

I expected to get resistance from her, but to my surprise, she
smiled and acted grateful to have a direction. When she was
ready, we opened the college catalog again and I asked her to
explain how to graduate. When she used technical terms, like
"GE" units, I asked her to explain what they meant. If she did
not know, we looked into the catalog together and found the
answer. I used the same strategy with each of our four kids after
they graduated from High School.

Since they were all aligned to what the college offered them and
expected from them, they all graduated from college—three of
them graduating in four years.

There is no substitute for aligning yourself with the plan.

Prayer in Three Steps

God wants to hear from us and He wants to grant our requests. He has included a number of passages in the Bible to help us know how to pray in a way He can answer.

There are basically three steps in prayer:

1. Align with God

2. Ask for what you want

3. Prepare to receive it

1. There are three steps in prayer:

_____

_____

_____

When you first begin, that is all you need to know to pray to our heavenly Father. As you want to get more effective praying, begin to explore each of these steps in more detail. As some of the concepts like *Abiding* or *Forgiving* start making sense to you, begin to incorporate them in your prayers.

Expand gradually. Do not let yourself be overwhelmed with the details, but progress fast enough to keep yourself challenged. Prayer is simple enough that anyone can do it and powerful enough to challenge the most proficient to new heights.

2. Prayer is simple enough that

_____

There is no lack of challenge when tapping the potential of prayer. Jesus said if we prayed with faith the size of a mustard seed, we could move a mountain from here to there and that nothing would be impossible for us. *(Matthew 17:20)*

We all have needs. As God goes around causing all things to work together for good *(Romans 8:28)* He loves to incorporate answers to the prayers we make.

The better we learn to pray, the more God is able to answer our prayers.

Step 1: Align with God

This is the step where we make a conscious effort to connect with God and see things from His point of view. This will help us align our wants to God's wants and recognize God's answers when they come.

> 3. This is the step where we
>
> _____

This alignment step is described in many ways in the Bible. The following sections will cover the most important ones. You shouldn't feel the need to tackle all of these at once. Just look them over and explore one or two that will challenge your current prayer life.

Remember, the goal of *Step 1* is to connect with God and start to see things from His perspective.

In Jesus' Name

In *John 16:23* the Bible says that if we ask anything in the name of Jesus, we will receive it.

> John 16:23 *"Truly, truly, I say to you, if you ask the Father for anything **in My name**, He will give it to you. (NASB)*

This means that as we talk to a God, if we are praying in Jesus' name, we recognize that there is only one reason a sinful human being can speak directly with a sinless holy God—because Jesus paid for our sins and clothes us with righteousness.

4. We will receive anything we ask for when we ask

   _____

5. Praying *In Jesus Name* means to approach God recognizing that

   _____

The only reason we have access to God is because of what Jesus did. So we approach God with the name of Jesus on our lips understanding that He made this access possible.

God wants us to pray in Jesus' name.

According to God's Will

Another description of how to align with God for effective prayer is to ask for what God wants to give us. Notice *1 John 5:14-15.*

> *1 John 5:14-15 This is the confidence which we have before Him, that, if we ask anything **according to His will**, He hears us. And if we know that He hears us [in] whatever we ask, we know that we have the requests which we have asked from Him. (NASB)*

There are many things that God has promised and wants to give us. We just have to get on the same page. He really loves it when we are so aligned with Him that what we want is what He wants to give us.

---

6. Praying *According to God's Will* is to ask for what God already wants

_____

Bible prayers are the easiest way to be sure we are asking for things according to His will. There are three Bible prayers I [D] like to pray back to God during my time with Him. It has been amazing to see how well this simple activity has aligned my thinking with His values.

---

7. The easiest way to pray *According to God's Will* is to pray

_____

The first prayer is from *Ephesians 1:17-21* which I have paraphrased the way I pray it.

> "Please give me a spirit of wisdom and revelation in the knowledge of You. May the eyes of my heart be enlightened so I will know what is the hope of Your calling, the riches of the glory of Your inheritance to the saints, and what is the surpassing greatness of Your power toward us who believe. You used this power when You raised Christ from the dead and seated Him at Your right hand in heaven, far above all rule and authority, power and dominion" (paraphrased from *Ephesians 1:17-21* NIV)

The second prayer is from *Ephesians 3:14-20.*

> "I bow my knees before You Father, from whom every family in heaven and on earth derives its name. Please grant me, according to the riches of Your glory, to be strengthened with power through Your Spirit in the inner man, so that Christ may dwell in my heart through faith; and that I will be rooted and grounded in love, able to comprehend with all the saints what is the breadth and length and height and depth and to know the love of Christ which surpasses knowledge, filled up to all the fullness of God. Now to You who are able to do far more abundantly beyond all that I ask or think, according to the power that works within me, to Him be the glory in the church and in Christ Jesus to all generations forever and ever." (paraphrase of *Ephesians 3:14-20* NIV)

The third prayer comes from *Colossians 1:9-12.*

> "Please fill me with the knowledge of Your will in all spiritual wisdom and understanding, so that I will walk in a manner worthy of You Lord, to please You in all respects, bearing fruit in every good work and increasing in the knowledge of You. Please strengthen me with all power, according to Your glorious might, for the attaining of all steadfastness and patience; joyously giving thanks to You Father, who qualified

me to share in the inheritance of the saints in Light."
(paraphrase of *Colossians 1:9-12* NIV)

As you pray these back to God, it aligns your thinking with what God considers important and helpful. If we pray anything according to His will, we know that we have our requests in His time.

Forgive and Be Forgiven

To pray effectively, we need to be free from the distraction of sin.

> 8. He wants to free us from the burden of harboring
>
> _____

He wants to lift us from the burden of our own sins. He will not hear us if we are holding on to our sin *(Psalm 66:18)* and He stands ready to hear our confession of sins in prayer *(1 John 1:9)* and forgive them.

> *Psalm 66:18 If I **regard wickedness** in my heart, The Lord will not hear; (NASB)*

> *1 John 1:9 **If we confess** our sins, **He is faithful** and righteous **to forgive** us our sins and to cleanse us from all unrighteousness. (NASB)*

He also wants to free us of the burden of harboring resentment toward others. When Jesus taught his disciples how to pray in *Matthew 6:12* He included this as an important ingredient in effective prayer.

> *Matthew 6:12 'And forgive us our debts, **as we also have forgiven our debtors**. (NASB)*

Some transgressions are easier to forgive than others. For the hard ones, God wants you to consciously decide that the other person is not responsible to you. Turn them over to God saying, "Lord you deal with them, they are responsible to you." Otherwise you are stuck waiting for them to make amends.

> 9. When you forgive someone, you are resigning from being their
>
> _____

Don't worry about your negative feelings coming back. When they do, just turn them back over to God again. Eventually the negative feelings will die down.

Your most effective prayers will confess any known sins and forgive any people who have wronged you. When you "forgive" someone, you are not saying their offense did not matter. You are resigning from being judge and jury and allowing God to handle it. You use your energy to trust God to do the right thing, even if things aren't going your way now.

Abide in Jesus

The Bible describes prayer as coming close to God, adapting to what He values, and wanting the same thing. You let God rub off on you and ask Him for what you want.

In *John 15:4,7* God urges us to find that place and camp out there.

> John 15:4,7 *"Abide in Me, and I in you. As the branch cannot bear fruit of itself unless it abides in the vine, so neither [can] you unless you abide in Me. "If you abide in Me, and My words abide in you, ask whatever you wish, and it will be done for you. (NASB)*

The word that is translated *abide* means to remain, to hang out, to spend time at a place you don't want to leave.

10. The word *abide* means to

_____

This is what happens to me [N] every time I come across a hobby store. I go into the store. I relax and marvel at the airplanes hanging from the ceiling. I study the new radio control airplanes on display to see if they meet my need. But most importantly, I *abide* there—indefinitely. I never want to leave. Even after I go, the experience still lingers with me.

God says to *abide* in Jesus as the branch *abides* in the vine. A branch does more than hang out with the vine. A branch also is connected to the vine. In prayer, we are to connect with God as our source of strength and as the one to whom we belong. Just like the branch soaks in nutrients from the vine, we are to soak in how much He loves us. We are to open up to Him and linger there. That is the perspective of effective prayer.

> 11. We are to open up to Him in prayer and
>
> _____

Delight in the Lord

One of the most effective ways to align with God in prayer is to identify the qualities of God that you love. In *Psalm 37:4* David says this is an attitude God can respond to.

> Psalms 37:4 **Delight yourself in the LORD**; And He will give you the desires of your heart. (NASB)

God is your treasure. He is the one thing you can count on. God is asking you to treasure your relationship with Him as the most valuable thing in your life.

> 12. God is asking you to treasure your relationship with Him as
>
> _____

You delight in Him because you can always count on Him: He is holy and will always do the right thing for you. He is love so He will do it with love.

To delight in God means you are fully satisfied and pleased with Him. He is your treasure. It means you see Him as your security and you simply trust Him. You want His will over your own will. You have a deep sense of satisfaction knowing He will keep you.

13. To *Delight in God* means you are fully satisfied and

_____ with Him.

If you delight in Him, you see Him as all good, all powerful, and in charge of you and He will give you the desires of your heart.

Worship the Lord

As we pray and think about what the Lord is like our natural response is to worship Him. Jesus talks about our worship of God in *Luke 4:8*.

> *Luke 4:8 Jesus answered him, "It is written, 'YOU SHALL* **WORSHIP THE LORD YOUR GOD** *AND SERVE HIM ONLY.'" (NASB)*

Worship is our response when we get a glimpse of who He is and what He has done for us. If we just get an inkling of the magnitude of the inheritance God has prepared for us in heaven, we become filled with gratitude and worship Him in prayer.

14. Worship is our response when we get a glimpse of who He is and what

_____

God has sealed us in the Holy Spirit, placed us safely in Christ Jesus, He guides our footsteps, and has already prepared good works for us to walk in. He just wants us to cooperate, to trust Him, and to want His will and wait for it.

He has it all planned out. He doesn't want us to work against Him. We are to get to know Him and understand His great sacrifice for us. If we get a hold of that we will be grateful and cooperative.

As you explore what God is like in prayer, you will know you are aligning with Him if you find yourself responding in worship to Him.

Meditate on Who God Is

God values meditation. This is not the kind of meditation where you focus your mind on emptiness or oneness as is popular in some circles. This kind of meditation focuses your mind on what the Lord is like. Listen to David's description of meditation in *Psalm 1:2*.

> *Psalm 1:2 But his delight is in the law of the LORD, And* **in His law he meditates day and night**. *(NASB)*

God reveals what He is like in every part of scripture. As you have been studying Abraham, you have been making a list of what God is like. Meditate on those qualities of God surfaced from studying His word.

At the time David wrote *Psalm 1*, most of the Bible had not been written. The clearest unit of scriptures available to him was known as *the law*, which consisted of the first five books of the Bible: *Genesis, Exodus, Leviticus, Numbers,* and *Deuteronomy*. Now we have the entire Bible and there is value meditating on all of it.

Meditation is most effective for those who respond well to visualization.

---

15. Meditation is most effective for those who respond well to

_____

This is an opportunity to visualize what God is like by picturing Him with the qualities on your list. Someone who has the qualities listed here as well as the qualities you have added to the list from your study.

- God is slow to anger
  (Exodus 34:6)

- God's mercies are new every morning
  (Lamentations 3:23)

- God is rich in kindness
  (Exodus 34:6)

- God is Holy
  (1 Samuel 2:2, Isaiah 6:3)

- God always does what is right
  (Genesis 18:25)

- God is perfect
  (Deuteronomy 32:4)

- God is not needy
  (Acts 17:25)

- God is love
  (1 John 4:8)

- God never sins when He is angry
  (Deuteronomy 32:4)

- God made a way for me to be forgiven
  (John 3:16)

- God has my best interest in mind
  (Luke 11:13)

It can be helpful to focus on those qualities that are different from your parents. Meditating and visualizing these qualities helps to update your relationship with God.

Remember, if you are an adult, your world is not controlled by your earthly *Family Of Origin*. Rather, you live in a world controlled by your heavenly Father. His love, kindness, and strength define the context in which you live. In a very real sense, "This is my Father's world."

Besides visualizing God, you can continue the picture by visualizing yourself as God sees you and visualize the way

Jesus connects us to God. To visualize yourself as God sees you, there would be an image of someone that was worth the ultimate sacrifice to redeem them from destruction.

To complete the picture, introduce the sin concept. View God as holy and yourself as separated from Him by the presence of sin. Then Jesus enters the picture, pays for our sin, and wraps you in His righteousness. This help to illustrate that our only path to God is through Jesus which is what it means to pray in Jesus name.

Keep in mind that some people really benefit from visualizing concepts like this. If you *do* benefit from visualization, this can help establish your context as you come to God.

Each of these descriptions in *Step 1* have presented a dimension of how to connect with God during your prayer time. In some prayer sessions you will be more successful with *Step 1* than in others. Seek to increase your effectiveness with this step. It sets the context for the prayer session.

Step 2: Ask for What You Want

After you align with God, you are ready to bring your requests to God. A prayer session does not always need to include requests for what you need. From time to time, you may be in a very good place where you don't feel the need to ask for anything. But you are probably aware of needs that the people around you have. Learn how to effectively ask God to meet needs.

Just like in *Step 1*, this step includes several descriptions of how to ask for what you want. Each of these descriptions give you another perspective from which to view effective petitioning. Don't try to incorporate all of these into your prayer life at once. Rather choose something that challenges you and work with that for a while. Then try another one. Always aim to keep yourself challenged without being overwhelmed.

Pray the Promises

The first description of effective petitioning urges us to focus on God's *Promises*. Don't pray the problems. Pray the *Promises*.

16. Don't pray the *problems*. Pray the

_____

If you focus on the problem and just repeat it back to God, you are just rehearsing the problem in your head. No wonder you finish praying and don't feel too much better. Instead, find a *Promise* in God's Word that applies to your problem and pray the *Promise*.

For example, let's say it is getting close to the end of the month, you are running out of money, and the bills are still stacked on your desk. A common way to pray is to wring your hands and say, "Oh Lord, You see all these bills and I am out of money. I don't know what to do." As you continue to pray, you just keep repeating that in different ways to the Lord. At the end of your prayer time, you have completely rehearsed the magnitude of the problem over and over.

A better way to pray is to align with the *Promises* God has made concerning your problem. The Appendix titled *Promises* on page 257 lists a number of these Bible *Promises* by category. Under the category of *Need for Success or Prosperity* the following *Promises* are listed.

> *Philippians 4:19 And my **God will supply all your needs** according to His riches in glory in Christ Jesus. (NASB)*
>
> *Matthew 6:30-33 "But if God so clothes the grass of the field, which is [alive] today and tomorrow is thrown into the furnace, [will He] not much more [clothe] you? You of little faith! Do not worry then, saying, 'What will we eat?' or 'What will we drink?' or 'What will we wear for clothing?' For the Gentiles eagerly seek all these things; for your heavenly Father knows that you need all these things. **But seek first His kingdom and His righteousness, and all these things will be added to you."** (NASB)*

The best way to align with these *Promises* is to use your own words to pray the *Promise* back to God saying something like this.

> Lord, thank You for promising to supply all my needs according to Your riches in Christ Jesus. My hope is in You. Thank You that You always keep Your promises. (paraphrase of Philippians 4:19 NASB)
>
> Lord, forgive me for worrying about these bills. Thank You that You know what I need. Help me to seek You, Your kingdom, and Your righteousness first. Thank

You for taking care of everything else. (paraphrase of Matthew 6:30-33 NASB)

Praying back to God a *Promise* He has made, aligns us with what He has *Promised* to do. As a result, we move from rehearsing the problem to trusting a *Promise* God has made.

17. Praying a Bible *promise* aligns us with what He has

_____

With Thanksgiving

God wants us to be thankful as we ask for what we want (*Philippians 4:6*).

> *Philippians 4:6 Be anxious for nothing, but in everything by prayer and supplication **with thanksgiving** let your requests be made known to God. (NASB)*

If your kids come to you already grateful for what you have given them, they ask for the next thing in a way that makes it easy to grant their request.

When we come to God grateful and appreciative, it puts us in the perspective where we know God will do what is right for us because He has already been good to us. When our glass is half full, we feel optimistic about our next request.

God is really generous and doesn't mind us asking. He likes to give and He likes us to know He can give. He just wants us to come believing that He has our best interest in mind. Praying with thanksgiving strengthens our relationship with God.

18. God likes to give and He likes us to know that

_____

With Boldness

In *Hebrews 4:16* God encourages us to come to Him boldly in prayer.

> *Hebrews 4:16 Let us therefore come **boldly** unto the throne of grace, that we may obtain mercy, and find grace to help in time of need. (KJV)*

For some personalities, it is second nature to ask for things boldly but for others it is a very new idea.

Asking God for things boldly does not mean praying with disrespect. It means to ask with the assurance that God accepts you and that He does not get irritated. He wants you to say what is on your mind clearly, freely, and without hesitation. This is what *He* wants.

19. Praying with *Boldness* means to ask clearly, freely, and without

_____

If you have not tried praying with boldness, you will be surprised how clear your petition becomes. Give it a try.

With Persistence

God encourages us to ask Him repeatedly for things by telling these unusual stories about a widow pestering the unjust judge *(Luke 18:1-7)* and a neighbor who comes in the middle of the night for bread *(Luke 11:5-10)*. God wants us to keep coming to Him.

For some people, their *Family Of Origin Issues (FOOI)* can hinder their willingness to ask persistently.

For example, if you had a dominating parent who would never bend, it can be hard to repeatedly ask God for things. We might think, "What's the use, He has made up His mind." If God doesn't answer our prayer right away, we are tempted to fill in the reason from our past experience.

Why didn't we get what we wanted in the past? Was our parent uninvolved? Did they favor another sibling more? We assume God has not answered our prayer today for the same reason. But we are usually very far from the truth.

20. If God doesn't answer our prayer right away, we are tempted to fill in the reason from

_____

Instead of contaminating the present with past experiences, we should look to understand what God is like, and interpret the unanswered prayer in light of the way God is.

Sometimes, when you don't want to keep asking God for the same thing it can be a defense. You just don't want to get whacked for being irritating.

Other times it can be pride and a desire to be independent. "Why should I have to keep asking? He knows what I want." It is a disconnect.

The harsh parent pushes you away by saying, "Don't ask me again. Leave me alone." God pulls you close by saying "stay with Me, keep asking, be connected, depend on Me, I won't let you down." He is the opposite of a harsh parent. He wants to be close. He likes you to ask and stay connected.

---

21. God is the opposite of a harsh parent. He likes you to ask and

_____

One strategy is to tell the Lord, "I am going to keep asking You for this unless You change my heart."

One of the many benefits of a heart fully committed to God is found in *2 Chronicles 16:9a*. You can ask God for strength to encourage you when an answer to a prayer is slow coming.

> *2 Chronicles 16:9a For the eyes of the Lord range throughout the earth to strengthen* **those whose hearts are fully committed to him.** *(NIV)*

For example, when we put our house up for sale, we expected it to sell on the first day because it had when we bought it. But days and weeks passed without success. I [D] asked God for encouragement when it hadn't stirred any interest in the first month. He led me to the passage where Elizabeth found out she was pregnant with John the Baptist at about 90 years of age! I burst into tears and said, "What are you saying Lord, I'm going to be 90 when the house sells?" I asked Noel about it and he said the Lord was probably saying that the house was going to take "longer than normal" to sell. Well, that interpretation turned out to be right. But, God has a sense of humor. The house sold in 9 months. I wish I hadn't focused so much on Elizabeth's age so I could see the other possibility!

Pray God's promises. He keeps His Word. He will increase your patience and steadfastness as you wait, and your faith will skyrocket when you see Him keeping His promises to meet your needs. His solutions are always far better than our forced attempts.

With Patience

Waiting is very beneficial. This is how we develop patience and steadfastness—two of God's favorite qualities in us. When we know He will meet all our needs and it's a done deal, we know joy is on the way. In *Hebrews 12:2* Jesus showed us how.

> *Hebrews 12:2* ...*who **for the joy** set before Him endured the cross **despising the shame**, and has sat down at the right hand of the throne of God."*

Jesus knew joy was coming. So even though He despised the shame, He kept the joy set before Him and endured. When we are waiting, we would do well to know that joy is on the way. God wants us to have expectant hope. Are you aware of God's promises to you and the inheritance He has prepared? Is today the day when God's answer comes? It is just a matter of time before you see God's deliverance for you. Jesus was clear on the joy set before Him. Are you?

22. When we are waiting, we would do well to know that

_____

With Help from the Holy Spirit

It can be a great experience to feel yourself align with God in prayer. But it is important to realize that your feelings do not tell the whole story.

In *Romans 8:26* God says when you pray, the Holy Spirit interprets your prayers directly to God in a deep and effective way.

> Romans 8:26 *In the same way the Spirit also helps our weakness; for we do not know how to pray as we should, but* **the Spirit Himself intercedes for [us]** *with groanings too deep for words; (NASB)*

The wording used indicates that the Holy Spirit really cares and is going to great lengths (groaning). This is not a flippant prayer. but a deep heartfelt concern for us and for what we are concerned about.

So, remember when you pray, there is a lot going on under the hood. Your prayer's effectiveness does not depend on how accurately you pray. The Holy Spirit is translating your prayer and communicating with God with complete accuracy.

---

23. While you are praying, the Holy Spirit is translating your prayer with complete

_____

With Faith

When we ask God for things, He wants us to believe we will receive them *(Matthew 21:22)*.

> *Matthew 21:22 "And all things you ask in prayer, **believing**, you will receive." (NASB)*

Think of it from the opposite point of view. If your child came to you, not believing you really cared or had their best interest in mind, it would be a bad experience for you both. In the same way it is a bad experience for you to ask God for something when you don't really trust Him. It is also bad for God because He is dishonored.

This is not what God wants. He wants you to ask in faith knowing He loves you and He can do it. He wants a relationship of trust, gratitude, and faith.

How do you know that you are asking in faith? If you are asking in faith, it will makes sense to start preparing to receive your request.

---

24. If you are asking in faith, it will make sense to start preparing to

_____

Step 3: Prepare to Receive It

The third step in prayer is a reality check. This step identifies whether you were praying to God or just mouthing the words? If you were praying to God, it will feel appropriate in many cases to do something to prepare to receive God's answer.

25. If we expect an answer, many times there is something we can do to prepare a way to

_____

In the excellent Christian block buster movie, *Facing the Giants*, the story is told of two farmers who desperately needed rain. Both farmers prayed for rain but only one of them prepared his field to receive the rain.

Which farmer prayed for rain in faith? Well, the one that was willing to put his faith into action is the one who prayed in faith. Which one are you?

Faith is not passive. If we really expect an answer, many times there is something we can do as an act of faith to prepare the way for the answer.

By saying this, we are not suggesting that you neglect the responsible part that you play in the equation. If you have a ton of debt, it would not be responsible to pray for money then go out and spend further into debt as an act of faith. But, just like the farmer, there are often ways that are consistent with being responsible that allow you to put your faith into action.

God wants us to expect His provision and He wants us to do our part. Our part isn't that big but it is important. When we do our part, it gets our mind right and our attitude right. We start thinking more ideally. We start thinking more eternally minded.

Preparing to receive God's answer to our prayer gets us more focused on God's timing and provision, rather than just focusing on what we need.

Are you preparing for rain?

26. Preparing to receive God's answer to our prayer gets us more focused on

_____

Skill Time: Designing a Time with God

Now it is time to put together a time with God that will match your current interests and desires.

As you begin to think about what would work for you, realize that a time with God simply consists of two things: Bible study and prayer. Any strategy you come up with that includes those two things is a valid possibility.

As you consider what kind of Bible study to have and how to structure your prayer time, you are looking for what sounds interesting to you and what sounds challenging without overwhelming you.

Bible Study

Here are several possible approaches to the Bible study portion of your time with God. Look for something that intrigues you.

Realize also that you can take elements from two or more approaches and come up with your own strategy for studying the Bible. Or you can start out taking one strategy for a while and switch to another strategy. Just watch that you are able to begin simply enough to match the level of your current desire for God.

You are looking for something that intrigues you. If you pick something that sounds good for a while, then you lose interest in it, experiment with different ways you can change the study to make it more interesting. A *Desire-led* time with God puts a priority on adjusting the elements to fit your current desire.

Four Step Bible Study

If the four step Bible study method works well for you, then continue with it. If you are interested in studying Bible books from the beginning to the end (and your level of desire can support it) I would suggest the following order:

1. *Philippians*

2. *Galatians*

3. One of these: *Matthew, Mark, Luke, John*

4. *James*

5. *Genesis*

6. *Joshua*

7. *Psalms*

8. *1st* and *2nd Samuel*

9. *1st* Kings

10. *Proverbs*

11. *Romans*

This list proceeds from truth that is simplest and most directly applicable to the more complicated truth. It also provides a pretty good survey of Bible history and doctrine.

Your challenge will be to read until something strikes you and study that. How much you study each time will depend on whether you are in the New Testament or the Old Testament, in a story or in a logical argument, or if your are tired or rested. Most people just read until something hits them and go only as far as their time permits.

Notes

God's Personality

If you are a "people person" you may like the kind of study that goes through the Bible to discover what kind of person God is.

To start this kind of study, you can go through the gospels *(Matthew, Mark, Luke, or John)* to learn the personality of Jesus. Then you can study the Old Testament historical books to learn about God the Father *(i.e. Genesis, Exodus, Joshua, Judges, Ruth, 1 & 2 Samuel, 1 & 2 Kings, Nehemiah, and Esther)*. As you study, watch what God reacts to, what makes Him joyful or angry, and what He rewards. What kind of person values those things and rewards those things?

Notes

Topic

Another approach is to study a topic of interest to you. You can do topical studies on subjects like: heaven, grace, anger, or forgiveness.

To find the verses that deal with your topic you can use a Topical Bible or Concordance (described in the Appendix titled *Tools* on page 247). Or if you like to use your computer, you can use the search feature of the *Wave Study Bible*® to identify the verses. See page 285 for more information on this software product.

Notes

Biography

The *Abraham Workbook* is actually a biographical study of the life of Abraham. You could study other interesting characters in the Bible like: Joseph, David, or Abigail.

To find the verses that deal with your individual of interest, you can look up their name in a Topical Bible or Concordance (described in the Appendix titled *Tools* on page 247). Or if you like to use your computer, you can use the search feature of the *Wave Study Bible®* to identify the verses that include the name of the person of your interest. See page 285 for more information on this software product.

Notes

Audio

You can even use the time you are in rush hour to commune with the Lord by listening to CD's of the Bible read aloud or CD's of devotional thoughts from the Bible.

The challenge in this kind of study is when and how to include prayer. You could wait until you get where you are going and pray before you get out of the car. Or you could try praying out loud with your eyes open. Many of the Bible characters prayed with their eyes open. Closing your eyes just helps minimizes distractions.

If this kind of study appeals to you, as long as you feel challenged, it can make use of some otherwise wasted time in your day.

Notes

Prayer

The kind of prayer time you choose is highly dependent on what works best for you. Some people find it most natural to talk to God at the beginning of their time, some at the end, and some sprinkle it throughout the session. Some people spend a very short time in prayer and use most of their time in Bible study. Some do the exact opposite.

Try one approach and see how it goes. Adjust it as you go to fit what is currently the most motivating to you. Check the earlier sections of this chapter and choose an aspect of prayer to work on. Take responsibility for making changes in your approach to find what is most helpful for you.

Notes

Do You Have a Winner?

As you are choosing a design for your time with God, ask yourself the following three questions. Is your design...

1. Enough to challenge you

2. Not too much to overwhelm your desire

3. Something that intrigues you

27. You know you have a winning design if its enough

_____

Not too much to

_____

And something that

_____

If you can answer yes to all three questions, you have a winning design. If you can not answer yes to all three questions, adjust your design until you can.

If you make sure the amount of time and kind of time match your current desire you will be on your way.

Assignment 7

For Your Mind

Study *Passage 6* and read the commentary that follows in the *Abraham Workbook* on page 238.

Also, see how close you can get to formulating a plan of activity for your time with God.

For Your Heart

To change your desires and thinking, keep praying the verses on the reminder card on page 283.

Identify one aspect of prayer, from those presented in this chapter, that intrigues or challenges you. Give it a try when you pray as a way to enrich and deepen your prayer life.

"If you enjoy
your time with God,
you will do it again.
And if you
keep showing up,
God will change you."

The Authors

Chapter 8:
Pacing Your Growth

"We want you to carry these bricks around and stack them where the workers can easily get them."

The task did not seem very hard. All I [N] had to do is move some bricks. It was the first day of my summer job in college and I was hired to be an architect's assistant. The first day they had me working at the construction site.

What struck me about the workers at the site was how slowly they were working. I was young and strong and set out to move the flat of bricks with skill and determination.

The first 10 loads went fine. Then each load seemed to get heavier. I was determined to make good on my commitment so I redoubled my effort. But with each load, my loathing of bricks increased. By the end of the day I never wanted to see another brick. The other workers had not skipped a beat, accomplished a lot, and had great attitudes about their work.

My eagerness to do a good job had persuaded me to take a pace that was too ambitious, and ended up ruining the job for me. It would have been better to take a slower pace, like the other workers, and go for effectiveness over a longer period of time.

When you begin having a time with God, it can be very tempting to commit to an overly ambitious schedule. It is important to remember that lasting change happens gradually over time.

Denise's testimony is an excellent example how a modest pace can enable long-term growth.

Testimony

When I [D] was saved, I developed a very simple time with God using a small devotional pamphlet that I enjoyed and my walk with God was going along nicely.

Then after a few years I found myself in a complex course in Methodical Bible Study as part of my undergraduate work. Unfortunately, it was not a very good course and by the end of it I wound up hating Bible study.

After the course, I found myself in no man's land. I did not like the new Bible study methods, but did not feel I could go back to my small devotional pamphlet since I knew all the new methods. So I did nothing for several years.

Then I came across *1 Peter 2:2,*

> 1 Peter 2:2 **Like a newborn baby, crave pure spiritual milk,** *so that by it you may grow up in your salvation,... (NIV)*

This verse challenged my life. I had just delivered our first child and I did not want to be the kind of mother that just went to church on Sunday but never opened her Bible at home. This verse said I had a *Desire* for Bible study that was just as natural as a baby's *Desire* for milk. I remembered having that *Desire* when I first came to Christ. So I set out to resurface the *Desire* God gave me to be with Him.

For a few months I would stop for about 5 minutes each day and ponder the same questions you have on your reminder card (cf. page 282). Eventually I felt my desire beginning to surface.

Then I wanted to design a time with God that would feed my *Desire* without overwhelming it. What intrigued me was to learn what God is like. So, I decided to start reading in Genesis and read through the Bible noticing what

God did, what He valued, what He enjoyed, and what concerned Him. Sometimes I would read 1 or 2 verses and find something about Him. Other times I would need to read many verses. But I found this approach appealed to me and did not overwhelm my *Desire*.

At this point in my life, I decided my *Desire* could support three sessions per week on Monday, Wednesday, and Friday. Noon time was the best time for me. That was when I put my daughter down to sleep and I had the right kind of energy.

Through trial and error I had to figure out how to guard this dedicated time. I had been having my time with God about two weeks when a girlfriend called to ask me if I could babysit her newborn while she went to the doctor. I said "sure." I fed my baby and her's and put them down for a nap so I could have my time with God.

My daughter went to sleep, but her daughter started screaming. She was fed and dry and I feared there was no cure for her gas. I paced back and forth with her, to no avail. I reminded God that this was my time to meet with Him and that I *really* wanted to meet with Him, but if she continued to wail I would miss out.

I will never forget what happened next. All of a sudden there was *quiet*. I looked down and she was sleeping peacefully in my arms. A few seconds ago she had been beet red with veins popping out of her forehead. Now she was peaches and cream. A few seconds ago her face had been wet with tears. Now she was dry with one little tear drop in the corner of her eye. I would have expected her breathing to be ragged and shallow from all the screaming, but she was peaceful and silent. I put her down and had a wonderful time with God.

The next week, my friend asked if I could babysit again. I said "No problem." Once again I put both babies down for their nap so I could have my time with God. Once again her baby began to wail. I prayed the same prayer, but this time to no avail. I felt like God was telling me, "You say your time with Me is a priority, but what are you doing to protect it?" I had to suffer through the colic and miss my time with God that day. Protecting my time with God became my priority. No more babysitting Monday, Wednesday or Friday at noon. I was responsible to keep my chosen time viable.

I kept my time with God at three sessions per week for 20 years while we raised our four children. During that time it grew from 15 to 30 minutes, then to 60 minutes, then to 90 minutes per session. It is amazing what you can accomplish three times per week if you keep showing up. When my last child left for college, my *Desire* had grown to the point that I was more than ready to go to seven sessions per week. Now, if I miss a session it feels like I have missed a nourishing meal and I will try and fit it in some way.

Something else has happened over the years. When I first started, my *Desire* was easily shaken so the choice of time was very important. It needed to be in a good time. Now, my *Desire* has developed so that I can have an effective time with God in a range of time slots. But most of the time I still keep it in my ideal time of day.

It truly is amazing how your relationship with God can grow just dedicating a few days a week to meet with Him. Your understanding of who He is, how He leads and what He cares about all come into clearer focus. Dedicating three days a week for 20 years transformed my life. It was a modest investment for such a big payoff.

God Loves Small Beginnings

Often it takes humility to admit the true level of your *Desire* for God and start there. There is a temptation to worry that you should be further along. But keep in mind that our walk with God is not about us—our performance or our power.

---

1. To admit the true level of your *Desire*, often it takes

_____

In *Ephesians 3:16-18* God makes it clear that it is all about God and His love for us. It is not about us.

> *Ephesians 3:16-18 I pray that out of **his** glorious riches he may strengthen you with power **through his Spirit** in your inner being, so that Christ may dwell in your hearts through **faith**. And I pray that you, being rooted and established **in love**, may have **power**, together with all the saints, to grasp how wide and long and high and deep is the **love of Christ**, (NIV)*

Remember how you received Christ? In *Colossians 2:6* the Bible says we are to continue our walk with Christ the same way we began our walk with Christ.

> *Colossians 2:6 So then, **just as** you received Christ Jesus as Lord, **continue** to live in him, rooted and built up in him, strengthened in the **faith** as you were taught, and overflowing with **thankfulness**. (NIV)*

We received Christ in faith and thankfulness. When we received Christ, God gave us a love for Him. The Christian walk is not about us but it is about Him and the love He gave us for Him. In *Revelation 2:4* the Bible reminds us to not forsake this first love.

*Revelation 2:4 Yet I hold this against you: You have for-saken your **first love**. (NIV)*

God is reasonable. He is clear. He is asking us to put our effort into knowing and loving Him. The focus is on God and He is 100% OK with small beginnings.

2. God is 100% OK with

_____

In *Mark 4:30-32* Jesus used the example of the mustard seed to illustrate spiritual growth. The mustard seed was the smallest cultivated seed in Jesus' day. It was 1/20 of an inch—a pinhead. It has remarkable growth. The plant grows 10-12 feet high and the stem is the size of a man's arm.

*Mark 4:30-32 Again he said, "What shall we say **the kingdom of God is like**, or what parable shall we use to describe it? **It is like a mustard seed, which is the smallest seed** you plant in the ground. Yet when planted, it grows and becomes the largest of all garden plants, with such big branches that the birds of the air can perch in its shade." (NIV)*

God loves small beginnings. He created many nations with one man Abraham. He offered salvation to all through one Savior Jesus Christ. He propelled one roomful of disciples to change the world. God loves to honor small faith in simple truth.

Find the level of your *Desire*. Then be humble enough to start there. God has provided us with the *Desire* for Him and His word. If we nourish our *Desire* and lead with it, His word can *Transform* us.

Skill Time: Bible Study Tools

As you study the Bible, there are some reference tools that list Bible verses and Bible concepts in a way that make it easy to find things. These tools are available in the form of books or software. This *Skill Time* summarizes the most popular of these tools. If you would like a more detailed explanation see the Appendix titled *Tools* on page 247.

Books

These books fall into four basic categories. Software tools will often provide the same service as one or more of these categories.

- A *Concordance* lists verses by word. You could use this to find all the verses on the word 'grace' for your own word study.

- A *Topical Bible* lists verses by topic. You could use this to find all the verse on the topic of 'forgiveness' for your own topical study.

- A *Bible Dictionary* is like an encyclopedia. It explains Bible topics like people, places and things that are mentioned in the Bible.

- A *Bible Atlas* explains and maps out Bible locations.

3. A Concordance lists verses by

_____

4. A Topical Bible lists verses by

_____

5. A Bible Dictionary explains

_____

6. A Bible Atlas explains and maps out

_____

If you wanted to find all the verses on love, what tool would you use?—A *Topical Bible* or a *Concordance*.

If you wanted to learn about altars, what tool would you use?—A *Bible Dictionary*.

If you wanted to to learn about about the place called Ur of the Chaldeans, what tool would you use?—A *Bible Atlas* or a *Bible Dictionary*.

If you wanted to find all the verses on Moses, what tool would you use?—A *Topical Bible*, a *Bible Dictionary*, or a *Concordance*.

These tools are very helpful because they extend your experience with the Bible. They put you in touch with all the verses from *Genesis* to *Revelation* that address a particular topic.

Software

The computer has the potential to significantly extend your experience with the Bible. I [N] have categorized these software tools according to how you make use of them.

- **Web-based Tools** are tools that are designed to be accessed through a Web browser like Internet Explorer or Safari.

- **Custom Software Tools** are tools that you buy and install on your computer.

- **iPhone Tools** are tools that are designed to be accessed through an Apple iPhone.

- **Podcast Tools** are tools that are designed to be accessed through an Apple's iTunes software.

There is a wealth of software help available. If you just want to experiment with these tools, I would suggest that you explore the *Web-based* or *iPhone Tools*. These tools are free and can be conveniently accessed using a web browser or an *iPhone*.

7. If you just want to experiment with software tools, you probably should look into the

_____

If you are interested in using software tools, you will probably have a better experience with a *Custom Software Tool*. These tools cost money (very little to very much) and are more effort to initially set up since they must be installed. But a *Custom Software Tool* is not restricted to the confines of a Web browser. Rather it can streamline your study and adapt to your needs.

8. If you use software tools very much, you probably should look into

_____

One *Custom Software Tool* that was written specifically to help people as they have a time with God, is the *Wave Study Bible.*® A description of this tool is available on page 285.

Bible study tools can help extend your current experience with the Bible and give you the benefit of exposure to the entire Bible.

9. A Custom Software tool that is written specifically for the needs of someone having their time with God is

_____

Conclusion

Keep adjusting your time with God so you continue to enjoy it. If you enjoy it, you will do it again. And if you keep showing up, God will change you.

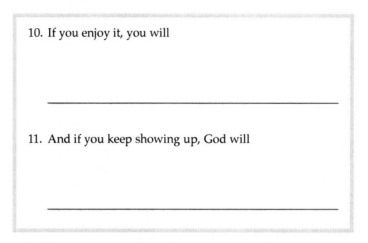

10. If you enjoy it, you will

_____

11. And if you keep showing up, God will

_____

God has given us a chance to hunger and thirst for Him. Will you *Desire* that and set your mind on it? Will you pray diligently for that?

Where is your focus? In *Joshua 24:15* God challenges us to face where we are putting our focus.

> *Joshua 24:15 "But if serving the Lord seems undesirable to you, then choose for yourselves this day whom you will serve." (NIV)*

Get to know God. He is the answer. Find how you like to spend time with Him and do that. Find when you like to do it best and do it then. It will grow. It will fill your emptiness and change your life.

God bless you.

The Assignments

Explanations

"Abraham
believed God,
and it was
credited to him
as righteousness."

Rom 4:3 (NASB)

How To Fill In the Panels

Following each passage are four panels that help you surface how God is speaking to you. Fill in the panels according to the instructions below.

1. Facts

In the *Facts* panel, make a list of the *Facts* you see in the passage. You don't have to list all the details. Just try and find the main points. You can use the same words as are in the passage. You will usually get somewhere around four to six *Facts*.

2. Lessons

In the *Lessons* panel, look over the list of facts and see what you can learn from the passage.

- Is there an example to follow?
- Is there a behavior to stop or start?
- Is there a comfort to accept?

Also, consider what you can learn about God from this passage? What does He value? What does He respond to? What pleases Him? You don't have to find a *Lesson* from every verse. Usually you will get one or two *Lessons* from a passage.

3. Challenges

In the *Challenges* panel, turn each *Lesson* you surfaced into a question that *Challenges* you. Listen for God to speak to you. He may not speak to you through every verse, but He will speak to you. You will normally get the same number of *Challenges* as *Lessons*.

4. Response

In the *Response* panel, consider what God is saying to you through this passage and decide how you will respond. Write out your *Response* as a two or three sentence prayer.

Be heartfelt and honest with God. If needed, put "training wheels" on your *Response:* "Lord help me to want this." Better to be honest and ask for help, than promise behavior you are not ready to keep.

5. Commentary

Now that you are clear on what you see in the passage, we give you the *Commentary* panel where we describe what we see in the passage. If you find something helpful in this panel, add it to your current understanding.

In this step you are comparing your study against that of an authority. If there are differences, do not automatically discard your idea. Rather, look at both concepts and see which makes the most sense to *you* and adopt that as your new understanding.

Example: Psalm 121

To get an idea how to fill in the panels, the following pages present *Psalm 121* studied using these panels. This is a guide to help you understand what kind of item goes in each panel.

More items are included in each panel than you would normally surface in the study of a passage. More are included to give you a better idea what goes in each panel.

Example Passage

Psalm 121:1 I lift up my eyes to the mountains; From where shall my help come?

Psalm 121:2 My help [comes] from the LORD, Who made heaven and earth.

Psalm 121:3 He will not allow your foot to slip; He who keeps you will not slumber.

Psalm 121:4 Behold, He Who keeps Israel Will neither slumber nor sleep.

Psalm 121:5 The LORD is your keeper; the LORD is your shade on your right hand;

Psalm 121:6 The sun will not smite you by day, Nor the moon by night.

Psalm 121:7 The LORD will protect you from all evil; He will keep your soul.

Psalm 121:8 The Lord will guard your going out and your coming in From this time forth and forever. (NASB)

1. Facts

I look up and wonder where my help will come from.

My help comes from God who made heaven and earth

God won't let me fall because He is always watching, He doesn't sleep.

He keeps Israel and doesn't sleep or even slumber.

The Lord keeps me and shades me at my right hand.

I am not attacked by sun or moon.

The Lord protects me from evil He is keeping my soul safe.

The Lord guards me now and forever.

2. Lessons

There are times we know we need help beyond ourselves.

Help comes from God Who created heaven and earth and is alert and ready to help.

God is constantly watching, ready to catch me before I fall.

He can be so attentive because He never sleep or slumbers.

God "keeps" Israel; God "keeps" me. Keeping me means He observes me, guards me, takes care of me, maintains me, preserves me, retains me in His possession.

3.　Challenges

Turn the lessons into questions that challenge you

Am I humble enough to seek help when I need it?

Do I go to God for help, or something else?

Do I trust God to "keep" me?

Am I willing to learn what God considers "falling" instead of assuming falling means failure?

4.　Response

Listen to what God is saying to you and write out your response

Lord, help me to be more aware of Your help and presence.

Help me see my relationship with You from Your perspective.

Passages

Passage 1—Hebrews 11:8-11

Hebrews 11:8 By faith Abraham, when he was called, obeyed by going out to a place which he was to receive for an inheritance; and he went out, not knowing where he was going.

Hebrews 11:9 By faith he lived as an alien in the land of promise, as in a foreign [land,] dwelling in tents with Isaac and Jacob, fellow heirs of the same promise;

Hebrews 11:11 By faith even Sarah herself received ability to conceive, even beyond the proper time of life, since she considered Him faithful who had promised. (NASB)

1. Facts

List what you see in the passage

Abraham went out by faith to receive his inheritance.

Abraham did not know where he was going

By faith he lived in a foreign land.

He lived in tents

Isaac & Jacob were heirs of the same promise

By faith Sarah conceived

Sarah conceived after it was unnatural to do so.

Sarah thought God was faithful

2. Lessons

Write down what you learn from this passage

Sometimes we need to obey God without having answers to all our questions.

God can do what he promise even beyond the proper time.
Our children benefit from God's promises to us
God works with faith

3. Challenges

Turn the lessons into questions that challenge you

Am I willing to obey God before I have all my
questions answered?

Do I have faith to believe
Gods will deliver on His
promises?
Am I willing to wait even
beyond the proper time?
Do I want my children to
receive God's benefits?

4. Response

Listen to what God is saying to you and write out your response

Lord, help me to believe you
will deliver the things you
promised me.
Please give my offspring
good inheritance
Please remind me that still
work even beyond the proper
time.

Commentary

"By faith"—those are the pivotal words for Abraham's success. Everything else followed that starting point. "By faith" he responded to God's directions for him to leave his home. He obeyed even though:

- He didn't understand

- He didn't have all the information

- He wasn't sure what he was doing

- He might look foolish

- He wouldn't have planned things this way himself

- He was leaving the "secure" familiar

- He didn't know where he was going or how long it would take to get there

He obeyed like a child. A child doesn't understand all the ramifications of the statement, "Get ready, we are leaving." He usually just believes that his parents are able to get him back and forth safely. That is how Abraham responded to God. He trusted God's character of faithfulness, competency and goodness. He figured God would not lead him astray.

Abraham was pretty comfortable in his home in Ur of the Chaldeans. There have been rich archeological finds from Ur that indicate it was a thriving commercial center during Abraham's time. It had several hundred thousand people living there in mostly two-story homes. The average home had 10-13 rooms with running water, central heat, air conditioning, and indoor kitchens. There were courtyards and fountains in the gardens. The interior walls were plastered and whitewashed. The city had a large library of 60,000 tablets, a school of philosophy, school of medicine, and a school of math. Commerce was well developed with ships coming from the Persian gulf to ports located at the mouth of the Euphrates. These ships brought diorite and alabaster used to make statues. The city was known for its jewelry engraving and weaving. They also had copper ore, ivory, gold, and hardwoods.

Nanna was the moon-god worshipped there. There is evidence of worship in the homes of that day with idols found in private niches in the home walls. From this city of idolatry God called Abraham.

Most likely, Abraham came from a family of considerable means. And now God was asking him to leave "his father's household" and go to parts unknown.

This unknown destination turned out to be Canaan. It had potential, but in Abraham's day it was undeveloped and nothing compared to Ur.

But this was God's selection for reasons only He was privy to. Abraham simply had to trust that God knew best. Even though Abraham wasn't exactly sure where he would end up, he was asked to leave a comfortable home.

I'm sure Abraham wondered about moving. Let's see—central heat and an indoor kitchen or God's best for me. hum.... Because he didn't hold onto what looked "secure", four thousand years later his descendants are more numerous than the stars in the sky. God kept His promise to Abraham even though Abraham did not live to see it. Right about now, I bet Abraham feels pretty good about giving up that central heat.

Commentary

But it was not easy. Abraham and Sarah had to pack their belongings, organize their group, figure out food, and travel on foot or by camel 1600 miles! It would take about three months to make the trip. I am sure they had their doubts. They had left their comfortable home and were living in tents. God's will probably felt unnatural and makeshift.

You will notice that halfway to Canaan they stopped and settled at Haran, which was approximately 670 miles from where they started. Haran was a city much like Ur of the Chaldeans. It would feel familiar. The Bible does not tell us if this was sin on their part to settle here. What we know is that God had told them to go to Canaan. Perhaps Abraham's father Terah was saying he was too old or too ill to travel, so they stayed in Haran until he died. Some estimate they were in Haran for at least a year. We don't know if Terah was keeping Abraham and Sarah from fully obeying God's will or not. What we do know is that loved ones can discourage us from obeying God's best for us.

Do you have a loved one in your life discouraging you from obeying God's will? Did you have great intentions of following God but find yourself settling half way in Haran? Are you afraid to set out again? Half way can be pretty comfortable. The only problem is that you might regret settling for comfort when you could have had the fullness of God's blessing in Canaan.

But God is patient, and after Terah died He issued His invitation to Abraham, again, to proceed to the land He had promised them. It was a second chance. To Abraham's credit, he responded again and left Haran for Canaan. Abraham's obedience effected not only his children's fu-

Commentary

ture blessing, but the course of the world. God is the God of second chances. Do you need one?

Abraham, did not obey God flawlessly:

- He didn't trust God to provide for them so he went to Egypt for help *(Genesis 12:10)*

- He lied to Pharaoh because he wasn't trusting God to protect him *(Genesis 12:11-13)*

- He told the same lie again later *(Genesis 20:2)*

- He had to deal with division and fighting within his family *(Genesis 13:7-12)*

- He had to throw out a disrespectful son *(Genesis 21:9-11)*

But Abraham failed without giving up. He kept following God. God values people who persevere in their faith, and have a sense of adventure.

Abraham needed both because God called him without giving him all the details. God's blessings can take time to unfold. Sometimes we need to be willing to let go of the "familiar" and let it get worse before it gets better. Abraham and Sarah were willing to look foolish, be unsettled, unsure and uncomfortable to get God's best for them and their family throughout eternity.

Do I expect God's will to be fully outlined, risk-free and comfortable? Or do I value faith and a sense of adventure? Once God gives us something to obey, then the rubber hits the road. Don't say you are moving to Madagascar to show your faith if God has not told you to do such a thing. Abraham obeyed God's Word. Listen to God's Word and be willing to follow Him without knowing all the details.

Romans 4:13 For the promise to Abraham or to his descendants that he would be heir of the world was not through the Law, but through the righteousness of faith.

Romans 4:14 For if those who are of the Law are heirs, faith is made void and the promise is nullified . . .

Romans 4:18 In hope against hope he believed, so that he might become a father of many nations according to that which had been spoken, "SO SHALL YOUR DESCENDANTS BE."

Romans 4:19 Without becoming weak in faith he contemplated his own body, now as good as dead since he was about a hundred years old, and the deadness of Sarah's womb;

Romans 4:20 yet, with respect to the promise of God, he did not waver in unbelief but grew strong in faith, giving glory to God,

Romans 4:21 and being fully assured that what God had promised, He was able also to perform. (NASB)

1. Facts

Abraham and his descendants received the promise of blessing by faith, not law.

Abaham belief God against all odd

Relied on God's promise

2. Lessons

Write down what you learn from this passage

We receive our blessings from God through faith.

We be
God will deliver on
his promises even if
in the natural we
can't see how

3.   Challenges

Turn the lessons into questions that challenge you

Do I think I receive God's blessing by my good
works (law) or by faith in Him?

De I believe God will
de as He promised
ever as I grow old?

4.   Response

Listen to what God is saying to you and write out your response

Commentary

The promise of blessing Abraham received was through faith—not through Law. *(Romans 4:13)* What does that mean exactly? Law is about how we behave. Are we keeping all the rules and measuring up to the required standards of conduct? Faith is about where our hope resides. Do we think we are good enough by ourselves, or do we look to God for help? Is our hope fundamentally in our own ability to please God (keeping the Law)? Or is our hope in God's ability to deliver us?

Can you imagine Abraham and Sarah's thoughts as they evaluated God's promise to them to be heir of the world? It says Abraham contemplated his own body and Sarah's womb—both as good as dead. Abraham was 100 years old but he did not focus on his age. He grew strong in faith by focusing on God's ability to do what He said He would do.

Abraham was not given the promise because of his ability to keep the Law. Abraham saw no evidence within himself or Sarah to believe God's promise. But, "In hope against hope he believed." When everything was hopeless, Abraham believed anyway, deciding to live on the basis of what God could do rather than on the basis of what he could do.

Hope is a free commodity anyone can take hold of. You can break off a little hope or help yourself to a lot of hope. The crucial issue is the recipient of your hope. If your hope is in yourself or another person, sooner or later you will be disappointed. If your hope is in God, sooner or later you will be satisfied.

You will notice that God gave Abraham many promises. Some were fulfilled in his lifetime like the promise of offspring. Twenty-five years after the promise, God gave

Commentary

Abraham and Sarah their son Isaac. But, God also promised Abraham that his descendants would be numerous as the stars of the sky or the dust of the earth. When Abraham died he had only eight sons. Four thousand years later the Jews and Arabs who descended from Abraham are as numerous as the stars of the sky and dust of the earth. God kept His word even though it was not during Abraham's lifetime. God's time frame is a lot broader than ours. So, what are some of the promises that God has given to us?

- *Forgiveness of sins:* *"If we confess our sins, He is faithful and righteous to forgive us our sins and to cleanse us from all unrighteousness." (1 John 1:9 NASB)*

- *Guidance:* *"Trust in the Lord with all your heart, and do not lean on your own understanding. In all your ways acknowledge Him, and He will make your paths straight." (Proverbs 3:5-6 NASB)*

- *Love:* *"For God so loved the world, that He gave His only begotten Son, that whoever believes in Him should not perish, but have eternal life." (John 3:16 NASB)*

- *Protection:* *"The angel of the Lord encamps around those who fear Him, and rescues them. O taste and see that the Lord is good; How blessed is the man who takes refuge in Him!" (Psalms 34:7-8 NASB)*

- *Second chance:* *"Because of the Lord's great love we are not consumed, for his compassions never fail. They are new every morning; great is your faithfulness." (Lamentations 3:22-23 NIV)*

- *Deliverance:* *"A righteous man may have many troubles, but the Lord delivers him from them all;" (Psalms 34:19 NIV)*

How would your life be different if you focused on God's ability instead of your own ability?

Galatians 3:6 Even so Abraham believed God, and it was reckoned to him as righteousness.

Galatians 3:7 Therefore, be sure that it is those who are of faith who are sons of Abraham.

Galatians 3:8 The Scripture, foreseeing that God would justify the Gentiles by faith, preached the gospel beforehand to Abraham, saying, "All the nations will be blessed in you."

Galatians 3:9 So then those who are of faith are blessed with Abraham, the believer.

Galatians 3:16 Now the promises were spoken to Abraham and to his seed. He does not say, "And to his seeds," as referring to many, but rather to one, "And to your seed," that is, Christ.

Galatians 3:29 And if you belong to Christ, then you are Abraham's descendants, heirs according to promise. (NASB)

1. Facts

List what you see in the passage

Abraham believed God which made him righteous.

2. Lessons

Write down what you learn from this passage

Righteousness comes from believing God.

3. Challenges

Turn the lessons into questions that challenge you

Do I think my righteousness comes from my good
works or from believing God?

4. Response

Listen to what God is saying to you and write out your response

Commentary

Wouldn't it be amazing if someone came to you and said, "I want to adopt you into my family and if you agree, you will inherit my fortune. I have done all the work. Your part is to believe me and accept my invitation." That is what God tells us in *Galatians 3*. If we have faith in what He has done, we are considered a son of Abraham. Just like Abraham, if we believe, then God sees us as righteous.

God told Abraham that "all nations will be blessed through you." I am sure Abraham could not understand how God would do this. He did not know God would extend salvation to the Gentiles (non-Jews). But, God was announcing the gospel in advance to Abraham. He told Abraham, in *Genesis 12*, that *you shall be a blessing* and that *in you all the families of the earth will be blessed*. The gift that Abraham passed on is the blessing of God. He was blessed in order to be a blessing. Sometimes we read promises and have no idea "how" it will come to pass—but God knows how. Our job is to believe Him.

Even though the promise was to Abraham, we are invited to share the same blessings when we believe. By faith we belong to Christ and become Abraham's seed, heirs of the same promise. Faith puts us on the road to blessing. Ultimately, the greatest blessing any man or woman can have is having a personal, intimate, love relationship with God. Knowing God, and guarding our relationship with Him is the most important focus of our life on earth.

At the end of my life I want to be able to say, "I loved God with all my heart, trusted Him completely, and persevered at whatever He gave me to do." How about you? If we focus on the goal of knowing Him, then we become blessed in order to be a blessing.

"Hope
is a free
commodity."

The Authors

Passage 4—Genesis 12:1-5

Genesis 12:1 Now the Lord said to Abram, "Go forth from your country, And from your relatives And from your father's house, to the land which I will show you;

Genesis 12:2 And I will make you a great nation, And I will bless you, And make your name great; And so you shall be a blessing;

Genesis 12:3 And I will bless those who bless you, And the one who curses you I will curse. And in you all the families of the earth will be blessed."

Genesis 12:4 So Abram went forth as the Lord had spoken to him; and Lot went with him. Now Abram was seventy-five years old when he departed from Haran.

Genesis 12:5 Abram took Sarai his wife and Lot his nephew, and all their possessions which they had accumulated, and the persons which they had acquired in Haran, and they set out for the land of Canaan; thus they came to the land of Canaan. (NASB)

1. Facts

List what you see in the passage

God told Abram to leave his country and family and set out for parts unknown.

2. Lessons

Write down what you learn from this passage

Sometimes God asks us to leave the familiar when
we aren't sure of the destination.

3.   Challenges

Turn the lessons into questions that challenge you

Am I clutching to the familiar when God is asking me to step out?

4.   Response

Listen to what God is saying to you and write out your response

Commentary

In the first three verses of *Genesis 12* God talks with Abram. He still talks with us through His Word. He developed a personal relationship with Abram. He asked Abram to do certain things in exchange for certain blessings. We have the same arrangement with God. Through His Word He asks us to do certain things in exchange for certain blessings. Abram's response was one of obedience.

God told Abram:

- Leave your country
- Leave your people
- Leave your father's household
- Go to a land I will show him

God promised Abram:

- I will make you into a great nation
- I will bless you
- I will make your name great
- You will be a blessing. All people on earth will be blessed through you
- I will bless those who bless you
- I will curse those who curse you

Abram's response:

- Abram left at age 75 from Haran
- He took Sarai, Lot and all possessions
- He went to Canaan.

Commentary

When God asked Abram to obey Him, He encouraged him by promising great blessing in exchange for following and obeying Him. God works the same way with us. He asks us to obey Him and He encourages us by promising His blessings for obedience. But, where are these promises of blessing to us you ask? The Bible is full of them!

If a lawyer wrote you a letter saying you inherited millions of dollars, but you never read the letter, you would remain clueless that you were a millionaire. You would never collect the money. Are we that way with God's blessings? He has written us a detailed letter, outlining His promises of blessing in exchange for following and obeying Him, but if we get distracted and don't get around to reading the letter we never get to collect the blessings. There is always a choice in life—stay with the familiar, or read the letter, obey it and go for the blessings.

God asked Abram to leave his country, his people, and his father's household. But, he let him keep his possessions and servants. God does not seem to mind possessions as long as we are not possessed by them. God seems to enjoy showering His children with gifts as long as they honor and obey Him above all, and are generous with others. We are blessed by God in order to be a blessing. If we are open to God and others, He can channel His blessings through us to others.

God is also willing to share His glory and greatness with us. He made Abram's name great. He made Solomon's name great. He made Moses' name great. He made Billy Graham's name great. He just wants us to remember where the glory comes from.

Commentary

When we find an instruction from God and are willing to step out and obey Him, remember He will show the way on a "need-to-know" basis. It is a "walk of faith".

Is there an area in which God has been asking you to step out? Abram was 75 years old when he began to seek God's will for his life. Do you think you are too old to respond to God's call to you? God picked Abram to show us that it is never too late to follow Him. How do we follow God when we don't know where He is leading?—By reading His Word and applying it to our circumstances. As you do, He makes His will known to you step by step.

"Being fully assured
that what
God had promised,
He was able also
to perform."

Romans 4:21 (NASB)

Genesis 12:6 Abram passed through the land as far as the land of Shechem, to the oak of Morah. Now the Canaanite was then in the land.

Genesis 12:7 The Lord appeared to Abram and said, "To your descendants I will give this land." So he built an altar there to the Lord who had appeared to him.

Genesis 12:8 Then he proceeded from there to the mountain on the east of Bethel, and pitched his tent, with Bethel on the west and Ai on the east; and there he built an altar to the Lord and called upon the name of the Lord. (NASB)

1. Facts

List what you see in the passage

Abram traveled to Shechem where the Canaanites lived.

2. Lessons

Write down what you learn from this passage

Sometimes God takes us through enemy territory as we follow Him.

3.   Challenges

Turn the lessons into questions that challenge you

Do I trust God enough to follow Him through enemy territory to get to the blessing?

4.   Response

Listen to what God is saying to you and write out your response

Commentary

There is something surprising about Abram arriving in the land promised to him, and finding it inhabited by the Canaanites! I bet Abram expected it to be a "turn key" property. Apparently God's will for us—our "destinations" in life—are not always clear, or even "prepared." Sometimes we have to work with God when we get "there" to clear the way and prepare it for His will.

God doesn't explain Himself, or apologize to Abram. However, in *Exodus 23:29-30*, God explains that He will drive out the Canaanites "little by little" rather than all at once. This was to make sure the beasts of the field would not become too numerous or the land would not become overgrown with weeds. God said He would wait to drive them all out until the Israelites become fruitful enough to possess the land and get their crops going. God has His reasons.

Reasons, or not, God's will can look confusing. There may be many obstacles. The coast isn't always clear and His timetable can be different than ours. When I am expecting God's will to roll out like a red carpet, it helps to see how it rolled out for biblical characters. God told Abram and the Israelites that He would clear out their enemies, but the Israelites were the ones wielding the swords! God does His work through His people. Talk about team work and adventure! How much do I want God's will? Staying inside watching TV doesn't break a nail or break a sweat, but then you won't have many stories to tell in eternity.

As I watch Abram following God, I see a pattern he uses to get direction. He stops, worships (builds an altar) and calls on the Name of the Lord in prayer. Pretty straightforward. Sometimes stopping is the hardest part.

"God's will
can look
confusing."

The Authors

Genesis 12:9 Abram journeyed on, continuing toward the Negev.

Genesis 12:10 Now there was a famine in the land; so Abram went down to Egypt to sojourn there, for the famine was severe in the land.

Genesis 12:11 It came about when he came near to Egypt, that he said to Sarai his wife, "See now, I know that you are a beautiful woman;

Genesis 12:12 and when the Egyptians see you, they will say, 'this is his wife'; and they will kill me, but they will let you live.

Genesis 12:13 "Please say that you are my sister so that it may go well with me because of you, and that I may live on account of you."

Genesis 12:14 It came about when Abram came into Egypt, the Egyptians saw that the woman was very beautiful.

Genesis 12:15 Pharaoh's officials saw her and praised her to Pharaoh; and the woman was taken into Pharaoh's house.

Genesis 12:16 Therefore he treated Abram well for her sake; and gave him sheep and oxen and donkeys and male and female servants and female donkeys and camels.

Genesis 12:17 But the Lord struck Pharaoh and his house with great plagues because of Sarai, Abarm's wife.

Genesis 12:18 Then Pharaoh called Abram and said, "What is this you have done to me? Why did you not tell me that she was your wife?

Genesis 12:19 "Why did you say, 'She is my sister,' so that I took her for my wife? Now then, here is your wife, take her and go."

Genesis 12:20 Pharaoh commanded his men concerning him; and they escorted him away, with his wife and all that belonged to him. (NASB)

1. Facts

List what you see in the passage

Abram went toward the Negev.

2. Lessons

Write down what you learn from this passage

Sometimes God's destination for us requires a long journey.

3. Challenges

Turn the lessons into questions that challenge you

Am I willing to persist and follow God in order to get His blessings for me?

4. Response

Listen to what God is saying to you and write out your response

Commentary

Abram is back on track, following God. God had told him to go to Canaan and he did. But there was a famine in Canaan. There is no mention of asking God for direction about the food shortage. It seems he might have done what many do in hardship—revert to fear and an "every man for himself" mentality. He left the promised land and headed for Egypt. He didn't go back to Haran, so it looks like he is still trying to identify with the Lord, but he had not learned to depend on God for everything. As they enter Egypt it occurs to him that Sarai is particularly beautiful and Pharaoh might want her. Rather than consulting God he looks to his wife for protection. He asks her to lie and say she is his sister so they will not kill him to get her. He says by doing this, she will save his life. He makes her responsible for his life.

Sometimes loved ones ask us to sin to help manage their fear. How about the alcoholic wife who asks her husband to lie for her. Or the abusive husband who says covering for him is in her best interest. Or the rebellious child who asks his parents to cover for him so he won't have a record.

Abram made Sarai feel responsible for him to motivate her to go along with his plan. Abram was looking for ways to save his own hide, but his sin hurt Pharaoh, Pharaoh's household and Sarai. Our sin effects others and will be found out in time. We don't need to "help" God solve a problem by sinning.

But, why did God protect Abram, the one sinning, and give the consequences to Pharaoh who was clueless? The answer lies in God's promise to bless Abram and make his name great. The blessing was not conditioned on Abram's behavior, but on God's faithfulness to what He promised.

Commentary

By giving Pharaoh temporary diseases, God protected everyone—Pharaoh wouldn't be "in the mood" for romance, Sarai would be safe and Pharaoh wouldn't unknowingly commit adultery. God kept His promise and He protected Sarai from harm.

It looked like going to Egypt paid off for Abram. He came back richer than he went in. But, looks can be deceiving. Among the riches he collected was Hagar, the Egyptian maid who would be part of Abraham's biggest heartbreak and sin down the road *(Genesis 16:1-16, 21:9-17)*. This wealth became a source of great tension and division within his own family. It was not God's blessing. Wealth does not always mean blessing from God.

Sometimes we are asked to go through hard times on our way to blessing. Our fear can lead us astray. It is tempting to use "street smarts" and "fly by the seat of our pants" in an effort to protect ourselves or those around us. Am I willing to follow and trust God through hard times to get His full blessing?

The Appendix

"We cannot do
great things
on this earth.
We can only do
small things
with great love."

Mother Teresa

Appendix A:
Tools

Books

1. Concordances

A *Concordance* lists verses by word. This allows you to look up all the verses that include the word 'abide' for example. This is very helpful when you want to find a verse whose location you can not remember or you want to find all the verses that use a particular word to study how the Bible uses that word. Here are the most popular *Concordances*.

- Young, Robert. *Young's Analytical Concordance to the Bible.* Hendrickson Publishers, 1984, 1206 pp., ISBN 0917006291, $12.58.

  This has been a standard work for many years. The English version is based on the King James Version. It is not quite exhaustive in that it does not list every occurrence of small words like 'the' and 'and', but it is very easy to use. It includes tips for breaking down words into their word families and gives some connection between the English and the original languages. I prefer this over Strong's concordance because it is easier to use and less intimidating for most people.

- Strong, James. *The New Strong's Exhaustive Concordance of the Bible: Classic Edition.* Nelson Reference, 1991, 1824 pp., ISBN 078526096X, $13.58.

  This is the other standard concordance that has been around a long time. It is exhaustive and it is based on the King James Version. It also has cross references to words that are used in other versions. It has several indexes that list subjects, laws, illustrations of Christ and names, places, and doctrines of the Bible. It comes with a numbering scheme to correlate English words to the words in the original language.

2. Topical Bibles

A *Topical Bible* lists verses by topic. This allows you to find all the verses on a topic like 'grace.' All the verses that apply to the idea of 'grace' are listed together even if the verse does not include the actual word 'grace.' Here is the main *Topical Bible* that people use.

- Nave, Orville J. *Nave's Topical Bible*. Hendrickson Publishers, 2002, 1616 pp, ISBN 091700602X, $12.22.

  This is, by far, the most useful tool for the devotional study of the Bible. Billy Graham said this was the most used tool in his library. It groups scripture verses according to their topic. The topics are listed in alphabetical order. Each verse that relates to the topic is written out in full under the topic. This tool is useful for studies on a particular topic or possibly for biographical studies.

3. Bible Dictionaries

A *Bible Dictionary* explains Bible topics. Even though the tool is called a *Dictionary* the articles are more like the articles in an encyclopedia. This tool is helpful for looking up unfamiliar people like 'Haran' or concepts like 'law,' faith,' or 'Christ.' Here are some options for a *Bible Dictionary*.

Butler, Trent, Brand, Chad, Draper, Charies, and England Archie. *Holman Illustrated Bible Dictionary*. Broadman and Holman Publishers, 2003, 1704 pp., ISBN 0805428364, $19.78.

This is one of several good Bible Dictionaries. It is colorfully annotated and is presented more like an encyclopedia than a dictionary. It is very friendly and easy to use.

- Douglas, J. D. and Tenney, Merrill C. *Zondervan's Pictorial Bible Dictionary.* Zondervan, 1999, 944 pp., ISBN 031023560X, $24.99.

  This is another good Bible Dictionary that is laid out closer to the way a dictionary is laid out. Merrill Tenney has a very good reputation for producing accurate and helpful works.

- Unger, Merrill F. and Harrison, R. K. *The New Unger's Bible Dictionary.* Moody Publishers, 1988, 1400 pp., ISBN 0802490379, $26.39.

  This is one of the 1st Bible Dictionaries and Dr. Unger built a name for himself by being able to condense useful reference information into a short and concise form. This is a classic though it might not present its material as beautifully. Dr. Unger also has written a very popular book called New Unger's Bible Handbook which is a small book but answers a surprising number of questions that come up.

4. Bible Atlases

A *Bible Atlas* maps and explains Bible locations. People are often surprised to see how much discussion is included in a *Bible Atlas.* Since the Bible mentions places that existed long ago, scholarship is often needed to identify the locations of these places. A *Bible Atlas* includes many of these discussions to explain how the locations were determined. A *Bible Atlas* is helpful for finding locations mentioned in the Bible like 'Canaan' or 'Mount Sinai.' Here are a couple of *Bible Atlases* to choose from.

- Brisco, Thomas C. *Holman Bible Atlas: A Complete Guide to the Expansive Geography of Biblical History.* Broadman and Holman Publishers, 1999, 298 pp., ISBN 1558197095, $19.78.

  This work includes beautifully presented maps of the different time periods of Bible history as well as a significant amount of explanation to connect the map to its Biblical context.

- Rasmussen, Carl G. *Zondervan NIV Atlas of the Bible.* 1999, 256 pp., ISBN 0310251605, $49.99.

  I am not sure why this atlas is so much more expensive than the other one. It is beautifully printed and includes some very interesting 3 dimensional maps. I do not have a preference between these two atlases.

5. Other Works

- Lockyer, Herbert. *All the Women of the Bible.* Zondervan, 1988, 320 pp., ISBN 0310281512, $15.99.

  This work surfaces each of the women in the Bible and identifies the scriptures that describe them. This is a very unusual tool and very helpful for biographical studies about Biblical women.

- Logan, Kathy. *Secrets to Always Answered Prayer.* eBook http://www.secretprayer.com, 2006, 156 pp., $27.00.

  Kathy Logan is a good resource for prayer encouragement and inspiration. This ebook is available on her web site. Also available is a signup for a free weekly email and Tele-Class that contain tips for how to pray. Although her web site may have a little too much merchandising enthusiasm for some, the message of her book and weekly email is quite good. It is rare to find an inspirational treatment on prayer that stays as close to the Bible as she does.

Software

1.   *Web-based Tools*

Web-based Tools are initially the easiest to use because you use them without installing any software on your computer. You just type the identified URL into your web browser and the tool appears. No software needs to be installed. However, web browsers were designed to do simple tasks like viewing pages. When you put the Bible into web pages and ask the web browser to perform complex tasks the experience becomes awkward. Web-based tools are best viewed as convenience tools.

* *Blue Letter Bible,*
 http://www.blueletterbible.org, free.

 This Web site provides a wide range of services to those studying the Bible. It gives you access to a wide range of Bible translations and Bible commentaries. It even has daily devotional thoughts and verses.

* *Bible Gateway,*
 http://www.biblegateway.com, free.

 This web site is also very helpful. You can pick a version, look up a passage, then look to see what commentaries have to say about the passage. The site also offers a Topical Index, a Keyword Search, IVP New Testament Commentaries and Matthew Henry's Condensed Commentary. The site also offers devotionals, daily emails, readings from Scripture, Spurgeon's Morning & Evening devotional, PDA/ Handheld tools, and something they call a 'studylight Lexicon.'

* *eBible,*
 http://www.ebible.com, free.

 This is like a Christian version of My Space. It allows you to establish an identity, interact with Bible passages, and send links to others that point to Bible passages you have found helpful. The site fosters a game-like atmosphere by assigning points to the ways you use the site and highlights the users that have the most accumulated points.

- *GodTube,*
  http://www.godtube.com, free.

  This is like a Christian version of You Tube. Anyone can upload their video to the site and the videos are indexed and are available for viewing. It seems to be a good source for illustration material for sermons or Bible lessons.

- *Bible.org,*
  http://www.bible.org, free.

  This site is maintained by the same group that launched the NetBible project. The site has a number of helpful items for pastors, small group leaders, and discipleship leaders. There is a library of sermon illustrations and articles that are indexed by date, author, topic, passage, series and language. The advanced search box for the dictionary allows you to select typical parameters for Scriptural searches and include the notes within the NetBible in the search.

2. Custom Software Tools

Initially *Custom Software Tools* are more difficult to use because you have to install them onto your computer. But once installed, *Custom Software Tools* provide a better long-term experience because each tool has been designed around a single purpose — the facilitation of Bible study — rather than being designed within the constraints of a web browser. If you study the Bible very much, you will have a better overall experience using a *Custom Software Tool.*

- *eSword,*
  http://www.e-sword.net, free.

  This downloadable software product is very functional and has versions for Windows, Mac, Linux, and PDAs. It includes Greek and Hebrew as well as reference works such as Barnes' Notes, Matthew Henry's Commentary, the Treasury of Scripture Knowledge, the International Standard Bible Encyclopedia, and Nave's Topical Bible, (the 1828 version), Thayer's Greek Definitions, and Brown-Driver-Brigg's Hebrew Definitions. Support for this free software is available at their public discussion forum http://groups.yahoo.com/ group/eSword.

- *The Sword Project,*
  http://www.crosswire.org/sword, free.

  This downloadable software project is an open source, GNU licensed, project. This software runs on Windows and Mac. The Mac version has its own subproject called MacSword for OS X and is available at http://macsword.com. This includes a 200 texts in 50 languages, Greek and Hebrew dictionaries, some commentaries, and Nave's Topical Bible.

- *The Wave Study Bible,*®
  http://www.wavestudybible.com, free.

  I [N] wrote this to be used during your time with God. It includes four Bible versions in parallel columns and provides training for how to study the Bible. It is quick, easy to use, and easy on the eyes. For more information see page 285.

- *Bibleworks,*
  http://www.bibleworks.com, $349 base price.

  This product only runs on Windows but it is very well done. It is aimed at the Bible scholar and includes features as sophisticated as automatically generating a grammatical diagram of Bible sentences. It has the best word study search of any product and can do searches on roots of words in any language. It also includes a support network and courses on how to use the product.

- *LOGOS,*
  http://www.logos.com, very expensive.

  This product has been around for a long time and is effectively marketed. It runs on Windows and Mac. It includes 3,500 electronic Bibles, commentaries, dictionaries, and original language texts. It is aimed at the pastor or professional clergyman who needs to footnote the sources of their material. I know many people who own this product but no one who uses it. It has many features but is very complicated to learn.

- *NetBible,*
  http://www.bible.org/index.php?scid=3, free.

  This is the kind of thing that warms your heart—scholars providing a top quality translation directly to the people for only the cost of manufacturing. This is a full translation of the Bible with stud notes done by many of the people that translated the NIV. You can download its text for a wide variety of devices without paying any royalties and it has an extensive collection of original language helps. You can use this tool as a web resource from this location http://www.bible.org/netbible/index.htm. The NetBible is also available as an eSword module, a Word document, or as a tree of Web pages.

3. iPhone Tools

- *Wave Study Bible, iPhone Edition*
  Apple App Store Search: Wave Study Bible, free.

  I [N] wrote this app to be convenient for devotional Bible reading, easy to use, and give convenient ways to compare Bible versions. It also has simple access to the Greek New Testament for people who do not know Greek. Three English versions and the Greek New Testament are included and the other translations can be added through the in-app store.

- *YouVersion Bible,*
  Apple App Store Search: Bible, free.

  This was one of the first Bible apps on the iPhone. It makes use of many Bible versions and is simple to use for quick reference to Bible passages. Comparison between versions is not as convenient as Wave Study Bible.®

- *ESV Bible,*
  Apple App Store Search: ESV Bible, free.

  This is a single version Bible app put out by the publishers of the English Standard Version translation. It is nicely put together and has the services that would be required for light Bible study.

4. Podcast Tools

- *OnePlace.com,*
  http://www.oneplace.com/, free.

  This is an amazing web site that presents a wide range of sources of audio messages in MP3 and podcast format. You can even listen to the current chapel messages at Dallas Theological Seminary through this site. The speakers featured on the site include Greg Laurie and Chuck Swindoll.

- *ChristianPodcasting.com,*
  http://www.tfc.edu/radio/podcasting, free.

  This site is another anthology of Christian podcasting. You can hunt down the podcast that is most helpful to your Quiet Time plan. This seems like a good source for those who are looking for ways to connect with God during the daily commute to work.

- *TruthForLife,*
  http://www.truthforlife.org/, free.

  At this site, you can select daily email and get a daily devotional delivered to your inbox each day. The site also has a signup for a daily podcast.

- *Doug Fields' Podcast,*
  http://content.simplyyouthministry.com/podcast, free.

  You can sign up for a regular podcast from Saddleback's Pastor Doug Fields High School ministry.

- *Drive Time,*
  http://saddlebackfamily.com/
  MediaCenter/DriveTime, free.

  Saddleback's Pastor Tom Holliday has recorded a number of 10 minute devotionals designed to take advantage of the time during your daily commute. The messages are available as podcasts or as a CD.

"If you have faith
the size of a mustard seed,
you will say to this mountain,
'Move from here to there,'
and it will move;
and nothing will be
impossible to you."

Matthew 17:20 (NASB)

Appendix B:
Promises

When you pray, align yourself with what God has promised to do. These pages contain many of God's promises and are organized by category. When you have a need, find a promise that addresses your need, then tell God you are trusting Him to meet keep His promise in the area of your need. Instead of praying the problems, pray the promises (cf. page 157).

Guidance

Psalms 37:23 The steps of a man are established by the LORD, And He delights in his way. (NASB)

Psalms 48:14 For such is God, Our God forever and ever; He will guide us until death. (NASB)

Psalms 73:24 With Your counsel You will guide me, And afterward receive me to glory. (NASB)

Proverbs 3:6 In all your ways acknowledge Him, And He will make your paths straight. (NASB)

Proverbs 16:9 The mind of man plans his way, But the LORD directs his steps. (NASB)

Isaiah 30:21 Your ears will hear a word behind you, "This is the way, walk in it," whenever you turn to the right or to the left. (NASB)

Isaiah 58:11 "And the LORD will continually guide you, And satisfy your desire in scorched places, And give strength to your bones; And you will be like a watered garden, And like a spring of water whose waters do not fail." (NASB)

Forgiveness

Psalms 32:5 I acknowledged my sin to You, And my iniquity I did not hide; I said, "I will confess my transgressions to the LORD"; And You forgave the guilt of my sin. Selah. (NASB)

Psalms 103:12 As far as the east is from the west, So far has He removed our transgressions from us. (NASB)

1 John 1:9 If we confess our sins, He is faithful and righteous to forgive us our sins and to cleanse us from all unrighteousness. (NASB)

Sickness

Exodus 15:26 And He said, "If you will give earnest heed to the voice of the LORD your God, and do what is right in His sight, and give ear to His commandments, and keep all His statutes, I will put none of the diseases on you which I have put on the Egyptians; for I, the LORD, am your healer." (NASB)

Exodus 23:25 "But you shall serve the LORD your God, and He will bless your bread and your water; and I will remove sickness from your midst." (NASB)

Deuteronomy 7:15 "The LORD will remove from you all sickness; and He will not put on you any of the harmful diseases of Egypt which you have known, but He will lay them on all who hate you." (NASB)

Psalms 41:3 The LORD will sustain him upon his sickbed; In his illness, You restore him to health. (NASB)

Psalms 103:3 Who pardons all your iniquities, Who heals all your diseases; (NASB)

Proverbs 4:20,22 My son, give attention to my words; incline your ear to my savings. For they are life to those who find the and health to all their body. (NASB)

James 5:14 Is anyone among you sick? [Then] he must call for the elders of the church and they are to pray over him, anointing him with oil in the name of the Lord; (NASB)

Trouble

Psalms 18:2 The LORD is my rock and my fortress and my deliverer, My God, my rock, in whom I take refuge; My shield and the horn of my salvation, my stronghold. (NASB)

Psalms 22:24 For He has not despised nor abhorred the affliction of the afflicted; Nor has He hidden His face from him; But when he cried to Him for help, He heard. (NASB)

Psalms 34:19 Many are the afflictions of the righteous, But the LORD delivers him out of them all. (NASB)

Psalms 55:22 Cast your burden upon the LORD and He will sustain you; He will never allow the righteous to be shaken. (NASB)

Psalms 107:19 Then they cried out to the LORD in their trouble; He saved them out of their distresses. (NASB)

Psalms 145:14 The LORD sustains all who fall And raises up all who are bowed down. (NASB)

Proverbs 11:8 The righteous is delivered from trouble, But the wicked takes his place. (NASB)

Proverbs 24:16 For a righteous man falls seven times, and rises again, But the wicked stumble in [time of] calamity. (NASB)

Jeremiah 29:11 'For I know the plans that I have for you,' declares the LORD, 'plans for welfare and not for calamity to give you a future and a hope. (NASB)

Marriage

Proverbs 12:4 An excellent wife is the crown of her husband, But she who shames [him] is like rottenness in his bones. (NASB)

Proverbs 12:7 The wicked are overthrown and are no more, But the house of the righteous will stand. (NASB)

Mark 10:7-9 "FOR THIS REASON A MAN SHALL LEAVE HIS FATHER AND MOTHER AND THE TWO SHALL BECOME ONE FLESH; so they are no longer two, but one flesh. "What therefore God has joined together, let no man separate." (NASB)

Ephesians 5:22 Wives, [be subject] to your own husbands, as to the Lord. (NASB)

Ephesians 5:25 Husbands, love your wives, just as Christ also loved the church and gave Himself up for her (NASB)

Ephesians 5:28 So husbands ought also to love their own wives as their own bodies. He who loves his own wife loves himself (NASB)

Colossians 3:18-19 Wives, be subject to your husbands, as is fitting in the Lord. Husbands, love your wives and do not be embittered against them. (NASB)

Hebrews 13:4 Marriage [is to be held] in honor among all, and the [marriage] bed [is to be] undefiled; for fornicators and adulterers God will judge. (NASB)

Titus 2:2-6 Older men are to be temperate, dignified, sensible, sound in faith, in love, in perseverance. Older women likewise are to be reverent in their behavior, not malicious gossips nor enslaved to much wine, teaching what is good, so that they may encourage the young women to love their husbands, to love their children, [to be] sensible, pure, workers at home, kind, being subject to their own husbands, so that the word of God will not be dishonored. Likewise urge the young men to be sensible (NASB)

1 Peter 3:1-7 In the same way, you wives, be submissive to your own husbands so that even if any [of them] are disobedient to the word, they may be won without a word by the behavior of their wives, as they observe your chaste and respectful behavior. Your adornment must not be [merely] external--braiding the hair, and wearing gold jewelry, or putting on dresses; but [let it be] the hidden person of the heart, with the imperishable quality of a gentle and quiet spirit, which is precious in the sight of God. For in this way in former times the holy women also, who hoped in God, used to adorn themselves, being submissive to their own husbands; just as Sarah obeyed Abraham, calling him lord, and you have become her children if you do what is right without being frightened by any fear. You husbands in the same way, live with [your wives] in an understanding way, as with someone weaker, since she is a woman; and show her honor as a fellow heir of the grace of life, so that your prayers will not be hindered. (NASB)

1 Peter 3:8-11 To sum up, all of you be harmonious, sympathetic, brotherly, kindhearted, and humble in spirit; not returning evil for evil or insult for insult, but giving a blessing instead; for you were called for the very purpose that you might inherit a blessing. For, "THE ONE WHO DESIRES LIFE, TO LOVE AND SEE GOOD DAYS, MUST KEEP HIS TONGUE FROM EVIL AND HIS LIPS FROM SPEAKING DECEIT. "HE MUST TURN AWAY FROM EVIL AND DO GOOD; HE MUST SEEK PEACE AND PURSUE IT. (NASB)

Children

Deuteronomy 4:40 "So you shall keep His statutes and His commandments which I am giving you today, that it may go well with you and with your children after you, and that you may live long on the land which the LORD your God is giving you for all time." (NASB)

Deuteronomy 5:29 'Oh that they had such a heart in them, that they would fear Me and keep all My commandments always, that it may be well with them and with their sons forever! (NASB)

Psalms 37:25 I have been young and now I am old, Yet I have not seen the righteous forsaken Or his descendants begging bread. (NASB)

Proverbs 11:21 Assuredly, the evil man will not go unpunished, But the descendants of the righteous will be delivered. (NASB)

Proverbs 14:26 In the fear of the LORD there is strong confidence, And his children will have refuge. (NASB)

Proverbs 20:7 A righteous man who walks in his integrity-- How blessed are his sons after him. (NASB)

Jeremiah 32:39 and I will give them one heart and one way, that they may fear Me always, for their own good and for [the good of] their children after them. (NASB)

Safety

Psalms 16:8 I have set the LORD continually before me; Because He is at my right hand, I will not be shaken. (NASB)

Psalms 27:1 The LORD is my light and my salvation; Whom shall I fear? The LORD is the defense of my life; Whom shall I dread? (NASB)

Psalms 121:1-3 I will lift up my eyes to the mountains; From where shall my help come? My help [comes] from the LORD, Who made heaven and earth. He will not allow your foot to slip; He who keeps you will not slumber. (NASB)

Proverbs 1:33 "But he who listens to me shall live securely And will be at ease from the dread of evil." (NASB)

Proverbs 18:10 The name of the LORD is a strong tower; The righteous runs into it and is safe. (NASB)

Need for Success or Prosperity

Deuteronomy 28:11 "The LORD will make you abound in prosperity, in the offspring of your body and in the offspring of your beast and in the produce of your ground, in the land which the LORD swore to your fathers to give you." (NASB)

Psalms 1:3   He will be like a tree [firmly] planted by streams of water, Which yields its fruit in its season And its leaf does not wither; And in whatever he does, he prospers. (NASB)

Psalms 57:2   I will cry to God Most High, To God who accomplishes [all things] for me. (NASB)

Proverbs 8:18   "Riches and honor are with me [wisdom], Enduring wealth and righteousness." (NASB)

Proverbs 10:22   It is the blessing of the LORD that makes rich, And He adds no sorrow to it. (NASB)

Proverbs 15:6   Great wealth is [in] the house of the righteous, But trouble is in the income of the wicked. (NASB)

Joel 2:26   "You will have plenty to eat and be satisfied And praise the name of the LORD your God, Who has dealt wondrously with you; Then My people will never be put to shame." (NASB)

Matthew 6:25-26   "For this reason I say to you, do not be worried about your life, [as to] what you will eat or what you will drink; nor for your body, [as to] what you will put on. Is not life more than food, and the body more than clothing? Look at the birds of the air, that they do not sow, nor reap nor gather into barns, and [yet] your heavenly Father feeds them. Are you not worth much more than they?" (NASB)

Matthew 6:30-33   "But if God so clothes the grass of the field, which is [alive] today and tomorrow is thrown into the furnace, [will He] not much more [clothe] you? You of little faith! Do not worry then, saying, 'What will we eat?' or 'What will we drink?' or 'What will we wear for clothing?' For the Gentiles eagerly seek all these things; for your heavenly Father knows that you need all these things. But seek first His kingdom and His righteousness, and all these things will be added to you. (NASB)

Philippians 4:19   And my God will supply all your needs according to His riches in glory in Christ Jesus. (NASB)

God Keeps His Promises

Numbers 23:19 "God is not a man, that He should lie, Nor a son of man, that He should repent; Has He said, and will He not do it? Or has He spoken, and will He not make it good? (NASB)

Joshua 23:14 "Now behold, today I am going the way of all the earth, and you know in all your hearts and in all your souls that not one word of all the good words which the LORD your God spoke concerning you has failed; all have been fulfilled for you, not one of them has failed. (NASB)

1 Kings 8:56 "Blessed be the LORD, who has given rest to His people Israel, according to all that He promised; not one word has failed of all His good promise, which He promised through Moses His servant. (NASB)

Romans 4:21 and being fully assured that what God had promised, He was able also to perform. (NASB)

Hebrews 10:23 Let us hold fast the confession of our hope without wavering, for He who promised is faithful; (NASB)

"The LORD'S
lovingkindnesses
indeed never cease,
For His compassions
never fail."

Lamentations 3:22 (NASB)

The Book

The Book Chapter 1

Desire-led or Discipline-led?

1. <u>Desire-led</u>   <u>Discipline-led</u>

Skill Time: Learning to See

2. <u>See</u>

Cartoon Strip

- One of them is fishing
- They look bored
- The boys look about High School age
- One has a cowboy hat
- The one fishing seems to be more into sports (fishing pole and flippers)
- The one with the cowboy hat may be a son of a farmer
- They appear to be in a very slow moving environment
- One of them owns a frog.
- Their idea of entertainment is a frog jumping competition
- They may live in a rural town (choice of entertainment, frog owner)
- It looks hot where they are.

Bible Passage (*1 John 4:18-19*)

- He is contrasting fear and love
- The 2 can not exist together
- Perfect love removes fear
- You fear because of the threat of punishment
- Love removes punishment
- God loves us
- God was the 1st one to love
- We respond in kind

Assignment 1 (*Philippians 1:9-11*)

- Love should grow in discernment
- So that we will like excellent things
- So that we will be sincere and blameless
- We will be filled with fruit of righteousness
- Fruit comes from Jesus
- Fruit gives God glory and praise

The Book Chapter 2

Desire Killer: Deceitful Desires

1. <u>To lie "</u>
2. <u>Does not deliver</u>
3. <u>The path to God</u>
4. <u>Fulfillment</u>   <u>Numb you</u>
5. <u>From God</u>
6. <u>Grow</u>

What Do You Want?

7. <u>Hesitating</u>
8. <u>Effort</u>

Skill Time: Facts

9. <u>See</u>
10. <u>Withhold judgement</u>
11. <u>See</u>

Skill Time: Lessons

12. <u>Learned</u>
13. <u>Unusual to you</u>
14. <u>Learn something from it</u>

Skill Time: Challenges

15. <u>My life</u>
16. <u>Lessons</u>

Skill Time: Response

17. <u>Respond to God</u>

The Book Chapter 3

How We Think Effects How We Feel

1. <u>The alarm clock rings</u>   <u>Cookie</u>

How We Think Effects How We Grow

2. <u>Transform us</u>
3. <u>Away from God</u>
4. <u>Transform us</u>
5. <u>Mind transplant</u>
6. <u>From God's point of view</u>
7. <u>Thoughts disobedient to Christ</u>

Desire Killer: Futile Thinking

8. <u>Futile Thinking</u>
9. <u>Nowhere</u>

Skill Time Finding the Lesson:

10. <u>Lesson</u>

11. <u>Clues</u>

12. <u>Different points of view</u>

13. <u>Authors</u>   <u>Recipients</u>

14. <u>What God is like</u>

The Book Chapter 4

Running from the Help

1. <u>Independence from God</u>

2. <u>God's mercy</u>

God's Pattern for Helping

3. <u>Took</u>   <u>Blessed</u>   <u>Broke</u>   <u>Gave</u>

4. <u>Took</u>   <u>Blessed</u>   <u>Broke</u>   <u>Gave</u>

5. <u>Takes</u>   <u>Blesses</u>   <u>Breaks</u>   <u>Gives</u>

Desire Killer: Taking Offense

6. <u>Deceitful Desires</u>   <u>Futile Thinking</u>   <u>Taking Offense</u>

7. <u>All the information</u>   <u>Take that thought captive</u>

Skill Time: Answering Your Questions

8. <u>What you don't understand</u>

9. <u>What you do understand</u>

10. <u>Pray for wisdom</u>

11. <u>Possible answers</u>

12. <u>Each answer</u>

13. <u>The support</u>

14. <u>Authority</u>

The Book Chapter 5

Family of Origin Issues

1. <u>You grew up in</u>

2. <u>18 years old</u>

3. <u>Your job</u>

Family of Origin Issues and Bible Study

4. <u>The Bible</u>

5. <u>Flaws</u>

Get to Know God

6. <u>Get to know God</u>

Identify How God Differs From Your Parents

7. <u>Of our parents</u>

Skill Time: Transformation by Imitation

8. <u>Over time</u>

9. <u>Watch</u>

The Book Chapter 6

Biblical Comfort Zone Examples

1. _Comfort_   Pleasure
2. _Power_

Introverts and Extroverts

3. _Project_
4. _Introject_
5. _Responsibility_   Word   Confess
6. _Angry_
7. _Humility_

Get to Know God

8. _Compassionate_
9. _Comfort_
10. _Practice_

Skill Time: Finding the Time

11. _Immovable_
12. _Wipe your schedule clean_   Time of Day
13. _Desire to study the Bible_
14. _Around it_

The Book Chapter 7

Prayer in Three Steps

1. _Align with God_   Ask for what you want   Prepare to receive it
2. _Anyone can do it_

Step 1: Align with God

3. _Connect with God_
4. _In Jesus name_
5. _He made it all possible_
6. _To give us_
7. _Bible prayers back to God_
8. _Resentment toward others_
9. _Judge and jury_
10. _To remain_
11. _Linger there_
12. _The most valuable thing in your life_
13. _Pleased_
14. _He has done for us_
15. _Visualization_

Step 2: Ask for What You Want

16. _Promises_

17. <u>Already promised to do</u>
18. <u>He can give</u>
19. <u>Hesitation</u>
20. <u>Our past experience</u>
21. <u>Stay connected</u>
22. <u>Joy is on the way</u>
23. <u>Accuracy</u>
24. <u>Receive your request</u>

Step 3: Prepare to Receive It

25. <u>Receive God's answer</u>
26. <u>God's timing and provision</u>

Skill Time: Designing a Time with God

27. <u>To challenge you</u>   <u>Overwhelm your desire</u>   <u>Intrigues you</u>

The Book Chapter 8

God Loves Small Beginnings

1. <u>Humility</u>
2. <u>Small beginnings</u>

Skill Time: Bible Study Tools

3. <u>Word</u>
4. <u>Topic</u>
5. <u>Bible topics</u>
6. <u>Bible locations</u>
7. <u>Web-based Tools</u>
8. <u>Custom Software Tools</u>
9. <u>Wave Study Bible®</u>

Conclusion

10. <u>Do it again</u>
11. <u>Change you</u>

The Assignments

The Assignments Passage 1—Hebrews 11:8-11

Facts

- He obeyed God's call even though he did not know where he was going.
- He used faith while he lived in tents as an alien
- Sarah considered God faithful to keep His promise to have her conceive beyond the proper time

Lessons

- Obeying and following God requires a life of faith because it won't always make sense (Sarah in tents/pregnant)
- God's direction can feel unnatural and makeshift
- God is faithful to keep His promises
- God values faith, obedience and adventure

Challenges

- Have I responded in faith to God's leading?
- How do I gip myself of God's inheritance?
- Do I expect God's will to be clear, risk-free and comfortable?
- Do I value faith, trust, obedience and adventure?

Response

- Please help me to have the faith, trust, obedience and sense of adventure I need to have to fully follow You.

The Assignments Passage 2—Romans 4:13-14,18-21

Facts

- If get inheritance by law, faith is useless
- Abraham used hope to believe he would be father of many nations
- Abraham saw his and Sarah's almost dead bodies but did not become weak in faith
- His faith grew because God promised and Abraham believed and gave God glory
- He was fully assured God would do what He promised

Lessons

- Faith is placed in God's Word and character, not circumstances or our ability
- We can have faith in God's promises when there is no outward reason to have hope

Challenges

- Am I fully assured God will do what He has promised?
- Am I seeking righteousness based on good works?
- Is my faith placed in God's power?

Response

- Please help me to remember that everything moves from faith in You. Obedience is my response to loving You. May my faith be in Your ability to keep Your Word and keep me.

The Assignments Passage 3—Galatians 3:6-9,16,29

Facts

- Faith makes me a child of Abraham
- The Scriptures saw ahead that God would justify Gentiles by faith which was preaching the gospel beforehand telling Abraham "all nations will be blessed in you"
- Whoever has faith is blessed with Abraham.
- Promises were spoken to Abraham and his seed which is Christ.
- If I belong to Christ I am Abraham's descendant and heir of promise.

Lessons

- Like Abraham, I am justified by my faith
- Faith brings blessing
- I am heir of promises given to Abraham

Challenges

- Am I leading my life by faith first?
- Do I claim promises given to Abraham?

Response

- Please help me live my life believing You and claiming the promises You extend to me.

The Assignments Passage 4—Genesis 12:1-5

Facts

- God promised:
- Make him into great nation
- Bless him
- Make his name great
- He will be a blessing
- Bless those who bless him
- Curse those who curse him
- The whole earth will be blessed by him
- Abraham obeyed and left
- Lot and Sarai went
- They took all their possessions
- They took hired help
- They set out for Canaan
- Made it to destination

Lessons

- God asked him to leave his family, country, but allowed him to take his possessions. God did not mind him having things. He wanted Abraham to trust Him.
- God shares HIs glory and greatness--He made Abraham's name great.
- God reveals His will gradually
- God showed him the way
- God blesses those follow HIm
- We can get blessings by blessing those close to God
- We can get cursed by hurting those close to God
- God uses us even in later life

Challenges

- Do I need to step out in my writing or teaching?
- Do I trust God to show me the way?
- Do I expect God to use me as I get older?

Response

- Please help me stay close and follow You my whole life. I want to glorify You even in old age.

The Assignments Passage 5—Genesis 12:6-8

Facts

- Canaan was occupied with Canaanites
- God appeared to Abraham.
- He told Abraham He would give his offspring the land
- Abraham built an altar to God where God appeared to him
- Abraham went to a mountain east of Bethel and pitched a tent. He built another altar
- and called on God.

Lessons

- Sometimes our destination is not clear or even "prepared"
- God has a different perspective about blessings
- God might give the offspring the obvious blessings, but Abraham trusted Him for his blessing
- God's ways are not our ways—the land was inhabited (Joshua 24:13)
- God gives us the help and encouragement we need to do His will
- It is better for my children and future generations if I follow God now

Challenges

- Do I trust You when I can't see the way or whys of my destination?
- Do I trust when my perspective and Your perspective of blessing are different?
- Do I think it is Your will only if it makes sense to me?
- How do I commemorate Your promise to me?
- [plant a tree? Stickies? Joshua 22:26,27 Numbers 15:37-41

Response

- Please help me trust Your perspective of blessing and leading of my family and me. Please help me trust even when it is not logical by this world's standards.

The Assignments Passage 6—Genesis 12:9-20

Facts

- There was a famine so Abraham went to Egypt
- Sarai was beautiful
- Abraham told wife Sarai to lie and say she was his sister so Egyptians would not kill him
- The Egyptians noticed her beauty and told Pharoah so he took her into his house.
- Abraham was treated well for Sarai's sake.
- God struck Pharaoh and his house with plagues because of Sarai.
- Pharaoh called Abraham and asked him why he did not tell him Sarai was his wife.
- Pharaoh commanded his men to escort Abraham away with his wife and all their belongings.

Lessons

- Sometimes we are asked to go through hard times on our way to blessing.
- We don't need to "help" God by lying to protect ourself.
- Sometimes being in sin can look like prospering for awhile.
- Our sin affects others and will be found out.
- God protected Abraham because He promised to in *Genesis 12:2-3*. Not based on Abraham's behavior but on God's faithfulness to what he says.

Challenges

- Am I willing to follow You through hard times to get Your full blessing?
- Am I willing to trust You to protect me?
- Am I sinning now and it looks like it's working?

Response

- Please help me persevere and trust You my whole life. Help me get the fullness of Your blessing.

"Take the leash
off your mind
and let it run freely."

Dr. Howard Hendricks

How Well Do You See?

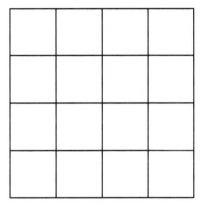

How many squares do you see above?

30 squares

As you look for squares,
look from different perspectives:
how many 4x4 squares,
how many 3x3 squares, etc.

Consider Bible passages
from different perspectives:
from the point of view of
different people in the passage,
for example.

**Without lifting your pencil from the paper,
draw four straight, connected lines which will
go through each dot only once.**

●　　●　　●

●　　●　　●

●　　●　　●

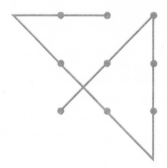

The solution comes from going outside the 9 dots.

When looking at a Bible passage,
we tend to get stuck in one way of seeing it.
Move outside that grid and view the passage
in new ways and from new perspectives.

"If you can see it,
God can use it."

The Authors

"Set your mind on
the things above."

Colossians 3:2 (NASB)

Appendix E:
Reminder Card

People who have taken the *How to Read the Bible So God Speaks to You* course have suggested that it would be helpful to have the seven questions described on page 41 and the three verses described on page 69 on a handy reminder card.

If the next two pages were cut out and placed on the front and back of a 4 x 6 index card they could become a convenient reminder card. A downloadable reminder card is available at *http://www.WaveStudyBible.com*.

1. Do I want to know God?

2. How do I want my life to be?

3. Do I want to do His will for my life?

4. Do I want to please God?

5. Do I want to know His heart and what He cares about?

6. Would I prefer my independence over His will and way?

7. It might change my priorities. What do I really want?

And I pray that
you may have power to **grasp**

how **wide**
and **long**   is the
and **high**   **love**
and **deep**   of Christ

that you may be **filled**
to all the fullness of God

Eph 3:16-19 (NIV, subphrases omitted)

Love the Lord your God
    with all your **heart**
    and with all your **soul**
    and with all your **mind**
    and with all your **strength.**
Love your neighbor
    as **yourself.**

Mark 12:30-31 (NIV, subphrases omitted)

God, have **mercy** on me,
    a sinner.

Luke 18:13b (NIV)

"Be willing to try
different ways
to study the Bible
until you find
what you love."

The Authors

Appendix F:
Bible Study on The Computer

The other way we help you learn how to read the Bible more effectively is by providing an easy to use software Bible.

Ever since I learned the original Greek, Hebrew, and Aramaic at Dallas Theological Seminary, I have believed that I could provide simple access to these languages through a well-designed software program. As I progressed up through the computer world in my day job, I worked on my Bible study software in the evenings.

When Denise and I combined our ministries I determined also to design this program to be the easiest software Bible to use. I didn't want users to feel intimidated or unsure how to make it work.

The *Wave Study Bible*,® is the result of this work. It is a free download for anyone with an iPhone, iPad, or iPod Touch. We also have a version for PC or Mac that is playing catch up and is not ready for distribution yet. An Android version is in the plans.

Easy to Use, Easy on the Eyes

This first version of *Wave* just has the beginnings of what we are building, but it accomplishes several of the ease-of-use objectives. My challenge is to make something that is so easy to use that a person with no Bible background will feel comfortable using it to read God's word.

Though the Greek is included in this version, I do not assume the user is interested in doing any language work. Rather, I focus on making this first version simply a great parallel translation Bible that is quick, easy to use, and easy on the eyes. Here's a video demo:

http://wavestudybible.com/wave-study-bible-iphone.html

Three English translations are included with the free download (King James Version, NET Bible, GOD'S WORD). The Greek New Testament is also included. You can also choose to add your favorite translation(s) from the in-app store. The store currently includes NASB, NKJV, NIV, NIrV, and The Message. The ESV and NLT will be available soon. All Bible translations are copied to your device. Internet access is NOT required to read this Bible.

All translations are presented in parallel columns along with the Greek New Testament and all are aligned on the current verse. The order of the columns from left to right goes from the most literal word-for-word translation to the most creatively paraphrased translation.

With this arrangement, you can read a Bible passage in your favorite translation, then when you wonder about the choice of a particular word in the text, you can swipe left to see how a tighter word-for-word translations renders the word or even how the Greek defines it.

On the other hand, if you are reading along in your favorite translation and you loose the trend of thought completely, you can easily swipe right to a more paraphrased translation and quickly pick up what is being said.

When we were limited to physical Bibles, the choice of which translation you carried was crucial because it was only feasible to carry one Bible with you. However, now it is no problem to carry around 10 or 15 translations in your shirt pocket or purse. With this new ability, you can choose to carry many different translations and use each of them in their strength.

The other real benefit of this kind of software is that it is very quick to find verses. By putting in a word or two you can remember from the verse, you are presented with all the verses that contain the words. Then with a few touches you narrow in and find the verse you are looking for.

Greek

The Original Version is the panel in the far left column of the parallel Bible columns. Just like all the other columns, it is aligned on the current verse. It shows New Testament passages in Greek and Old Testament passages in Hebrew or Aramaic. Each passage is presented in the language in which it was originally written.

To make sense of a Greek word, just touch it. Up pops a translucent window that shows the word's parsing and definition. If you want to know which Greek word a particular English word comes from, just keep touching the Greek words in the verse until you find a definition that makes sense. That's your word and the definition tells you a little more about it.

Then if you want to go deeper, you can flip over the panel and press the search tab. You will find (the lexical form of) the word you just touched already typed in the search field for you. All you have to do is press the search button.

Instantly all the verses that use any form of that word are listed for you. When you press on a verse, all 4 of the Bible versions go to that verse. So you can swipe over to each version and see how they translate your word—very easy and very quick.

This is called a *Word Study* and is the way the pros come to understand the meaning of words in the Bible. And you did it just by touching the word and pressing search.

Since the Greek New Testament was made available to our project for free by the kindness of its editors, Drs. Maurice

Robinson and William Pierpont, we have included it in the free initial download.

The Hebrew/Aramaic Old Testament (BHS) was licensed to our project so we will be making it available for purchase in our next release through our in-app store.

It has been a real thrill to see how many people have followed their curiosity to explore the Greek New Testament in *Wave*. I want this software to help people who are just beginning to read the Bible *and* help them go as deep as they want to go.

Training

Built into this version of *Wave* (and especially into the next version) are short *Lessons* that teach how to study the Bible. The *Lessons* are delivered in written and video form.

Most people would never believe they could just read a Bible passage and get something out of it. These *Lessons* demonstrate how to do that. So you can use your Bible, to learn how to read the Bible.

These cellphone platforms make personal Bible reading and growth more possible today than ever before. I don't know about your experience, but when I sit down and open a full size Bible to read something, it tends to alienate the people around me.

But now I can read as much Bible as I want, no matter where I am, without people getting uncomfortable. In fact, several people have caught a glimpse of the colorful panels in *Wave* and want to know what program I am using. Which, of course, gives me the chance to show them passages from the Bible as I answer their questions.

What's Coming?

This first phase of *Wave* is focused on the ease-of use features and on making Greek easily available.

The next release begins the second phase in which we add an iPad-specific version, the ability to take notes or create verse collections, and full *4-Panel* passage studies. We also will add the Hebrew/Aramaic Old Testament (BHS) and other popular translations like the ESV and NLT.

We want you to be able to read the Bible and capture what you see then share it with others. In this second phase we will also get *Wave* on all the target platforms: PC, Mac, Android, and the iPhone family. Your notes are synchronized between each of your platforms.

In phase three we bring out the result of decades of research on how to best connect the Greek/Hebrew/Aramaic with English Bible translations. It is like there is this huge wall that separates English Bible from the original texts. In phase three we give you a good way to jump that wall.

You do NOT need software to learn to study the Bible. In fact, you lose some features available in physical books. But with software, you gain the ability to easily compare multiple translations, to search to find verses, and to take advantage of moments during the day to remind yourself of God's perspective.

If you are interested in downloading this free app, use your device to go to the Apple App Store and search for *Wave Study Bible* then press the Free button. We would love to hear your thoughts. Send them to

support@wavestudybible.com

"All of a sudden
I felt the urge
to do follow-up work."

Dr. Noel

Appendix G:
More About the Authors

When we teach in person, we share more of our background story. For those who find this helpful, our story follows.

Early Years

Both of us were born in 1951, have been married since 1972, and have four grown kids.

We met in our Junior year at California Polytechnic University in San Luis Obispo, California. Denise was a speech major and had recently accepted the Lord through the Campus Crusade for Christ ministry. I [N] was a mechanical engineering major and became a Christian during my childhood. I had rededicated my life to the Lord in a little Baptist church just off campus.

One Sunday I was singing in the choir when Denise and her two roommates walked in and sat in the back. OK, so I found myself distracted by the glow coming from that side of the room.

At the end of the service, the minister invited anyone who had recently accepted God's gift to come to the front of the room. Denise came forward and I suddenly felt the urge to do follow-up work. I became the answer to her prayer for Christian fellowship and we were married the next summer.

School

We felt called into the ministry and left Cal Poly for Baptist Bible College of Pennsylvania. In our four years there,

I earned a Bachelors in Bible and taught classical guitar on the faculty. Denise also earned a Bachelors in Bible there.

Since all the good teachers at the school were from Dallas Theological Seminary, after graduating we moved to Dallas to attend DTS. All four of our kids were born in Dallas. According to our two year old, I attended the "Dallas *Theolaundromat* Seminary."

Both Denise and I tackled the challenging programs of DTS. She pursued a Masters in Bible but stopped half way through after delivering our twins. In Bible college I concentrated on Greek, so in DTS I completed a Th.M. in Hebrew Exegesis.

While in Dallas, I enjoyed a ministry at Dallas Bible College where I taught, Bible, theology, guitar, and Introduction to Computers. After graduation I also worked on staff at Dallas Theological Seminary.

Computer and Teaching

After graduating from DTS, I [N] had an interesting and significant twist in direction.

While I was working on the DTS staff they had a need for someone who knew computers. I had an engineering and programming background from Cal Poly and got the position. In this responsibility I eventually created and managed DTS's mainframe data center and started programming the *Wave Study Bible®* in the evenings.

After being out of state for 15 years the Lord led us back to our roots in Southern California. I got a programming job and advanced in the computer field. After a number of years I was a Chief Architect for America Online doing research and development. During that time, Prentice Hall published my book on Java programming and I taught Java programming at UC Irvine extension.

Depression and Recovery

For one reason or another I [N] had an emotionally difficult childhood. During that time I made coping decisions that were appropriate for that situation but not appropriate for adult life. When I grew up, I did not update those decisions and eventually they caught up with me. While I was working for Dallas Theological Seminary I landed in the hospital with a clinical depression. The three weeks I was in the hospital brought my life to a complete stand still.

During that time I had no idea what God was doing in my life. All I knew was, if I was going to get out of this, it was going to require a lot of work on my part. Regardless of my devotion to God, He was allowing these dynamics to shut down my life and the only way back was to tackle them head on.

So, with counseling and the skillful and kind support of Denise, I surfaced the flawed coping decisions made as a child and updated them. This was a difficult task that demanded all of my creativity and brought most of my ministry activities to a stop.

During this time, I was focused on emotional recovery, meeting the needs of our family, and my job. The little time I was able to give to ministry took the form of teaching people to study the Bible and programming the *Wave Study Bible.*®

After about a decade, things returned to an even keel and I finished my schooling by earning a Doctor of Education. I specialized in Internet-based learning systems which found their way into the *Wave Study Bible.*®

Psychology and Private Practice

After the kids were older, Denise went back and got her Masters and Doctor of Psychology degrees and opened a clinical private practice. Her specialty is integrating Biblical principles with principles of good mental health.

Wave Study Bible® Ministry

The first influence toward the *Wave Study Bible® Ministry* occurred several years ago when a young married woman in our church asked Denise if she would mentor her. She wanted to know how to love the Lord better and be a good wife. The material Denise delivered to the woman and a group of her friends was so well-received that Denise gave the course to several other groups in the church.

Then God gave us a special moment as we were applying the teaching of our church's course on spiritual gifts. We were trying to find a ministry that would make use of our gifts and the variety of our experiences. God stopped us in our tracks by suggesting that we combine our ministries to help people with their Bible reading times.

Denise's discipleship and psychology background helped address the motivational issues that stop most Bible reading times. My background teaching people how to study the Bible, equipped people with the skills to feed themselves.

When God led me into the computer field in 1981, it felt like a diversion and did not make much sense. But soon after I entered this field, God gave me the idea to develop software that taught people how to study the Bible. Today the Internet age has arrived and, the *Wave Study Bible®* is ready. It has been exciting to see how this tool has helped people study and share what they are learning with others online. What seemed like a diversion, got me going on a tool that was ready in time to leverage the resources of the Internet.

After the idea for the combined ministry was born, we wrote the book *How to Read the Bible So God Speaks to You* and taught it to hundreds of people in churches in our area. As we did, we experienced the kind of ministry we envisioned many years ago when we set out for Bible College. Now the *Wave Study Bible® Ministry* has grown to involve many people and has a wide outreach.

Our life has taken many turns and twists and has defied conventional wisdom. But, as always, God's path has brought us directly to His will and we are thankful for His working in our lives.

CPSIA information can be obtained
at www.ICGtesting.com
Printed in the USA
LVOW12s0209090317
526620LV00002B/225/P